# The Most Amazing Baseball Stories of All Time for Kids

*20 Inspirational Tales From Baseball History for Young Readers*

Bradley Simon

# Table of Contents

# Introduction

Picture this: the crowd's roar echoes in your ears, the smell of fresh popcorn and sizzling hot dogs fill the air, and everyone jumps out of their seats as your favorite player smashes a home run. This is what baseball is all about! Each game is a wild ride filled with cheering fans, surprise twists, incredible plays, and a wave of emotions that keep us on the edge of our seats. It's the joy of a stunning catch, the surprise of a trick pitch, the thrill of a walk-off home run, and the moments that create legends. But behind every play, behind every statistic and every victory, there's a story. This book is your ticket to explore some of the most exciting, heartwarming, and inspirational stories from the world of baseball.

Baseball, often referred to as America's pastime, is more than just a game. It's a thrilling saga of human spirit and athleticism. It's a ballet of precision and strategy, combined with raw power and speed. It's a contest where ordinary men and women become heroes, where dreams are achieved, and where every pitch, every swing, and every catch matters.

In this book, we'll step onto the diamond - that beautiful field of green where the magic happens - and explore the stories that have helped shape the game of baseball. From the early beginnings of the sport, to iconic moments that made headlines, to stories of incredible personal achievement that may surprise you. These aren't just tales about a game; they're lessons about life, character, and the human spirit.

Now, imagine standing on the pitcher's mound, a sea of spectators around you. Feel the weight of the baseball in your hand, the sunlight warming your back, the anticipation hanging heavy in the air. You wind up, let the ball fly, and the crowd erupts as the bat connects with a satisfying crack. In baseball, as in life, every moment holds the potential for something extraordinary to happen.

We'll begin our journey with Babe Ruth, one of the game's earliest and brightest stars, and relive his legendary "Called Shot" during the 1932 World Series. We'll discover that it's not just about the remarkable home run he hit, but the confidence with which he played the game, forever transforming baseball into a spectacle of suspense and excitement.

From there, we'll move onto Jackie Robinson's historic debut in Major League Baseball. His bravery in breaking the color barrier in 1947 was not only a significant moment in baseball history but also a momentous step forward in the ongoing fight for civil rights.

We'll witness the improbable victories and astonishing feats, such as the New York Mets' surprising win at the 1969 World Series, and Kirk Gibson's unforgettable home run in the 1988 World Series, hit despite his injuries. We'll cheer for Cal Ripken Jr., the Ironman of baseball, who played an astounding 2,632 consecutive games, proving his unwavering dedication to the sport.

Our journey will introduce us to the legends of the game, like Hank Aaron and his record-breaking career. We'll admire the grace of Willie Mays and his stunning over-the-shoulder catch, and feel the tension during the 1998 home run race between Mark McGwire and Sammy Sosa.

This journey isn't just about the stars of the game, though. It's also about the spirit of the game. It's about the creation and success of the All-American Girls Professional Baseball League, proving that baseball isn't just a man's sport. It's about the Boston Red Sox finally breaking their 86-year championship drought, reminding us that patience and perseverance can lead to amazing triumphs. It's about the strong bonds and friendships formed, like that between Lou Gehrig and Babe Ruth, which serve as a testament to the team spirit that lies at the heart of baseball.

Each of these stories offers a lesson - about the importance of believing in ourselves, about standing up for what's right, about never giving up no matter the odds. These lessons extend beyond the baseball field; they are lessons for life. They teach us about the importance of teamwork, sportsmanship, perseverance, and respect.

As we delve deeper into these tales, we will also see how baseball brings together diverse groups of people, creating a unique and unified community. From the cheering fans in the stands, to the players giving their all on the field, to the families listening to the game on the radio at home, baseball has a special way of connecting people. It bridges generations and cultures, creating bonds that are deeper than just a shared interest in a sport.

This journey will also take us to the edge of our seats with thrilling catches, like Jim Edmonds' outstanding diving snag, and heart-stopping games like the Boston Red Sox's victory in 2004 that ended an 86-year championship drought. We will celebrate young talents like Bryce Harper who burst onto the scene and quickly rose to become one of the sport's most celebrated players.

This book is a tribute to the grand game of baseball. It's a tribute to the men and women, the boys and girls, who have played this game, who have cheered from the stands, who have listened with bated breath to the play-by-play announcements on the radio.

The stories in this book are like the many innings of a baseball game. Each has its own arc, its own moments of tension and triumph. Each story stands alone, but together, they tell a bigger narrative about the incredible world of baseball.

As you venture through these pages, you'll discover that baseball is a game of moments. The moment when the ball meets the bat, when a runner slides into home plate, when a pitch is thrown with perfect accuracy. These moments come together to create an unforgettable experience that resonates with millions of fans around the world.

But baseball is not just about the dramatic moments on the field. It's also about the lessons we learn off the field. It's about hard work, determination, teamwork, and resilience. It's about learning to handle defeat with grace and victories with humility.

Through this journey, we hope to inspire you, make you marvel, and deepen your love for the game. Whether you're a die-hard fan, a casual observer, or a future star of the diamond, we hope that these stories fill you with a sense of awe, admiration, and a deeper understanding of why baseball is more than a game—it's a way of life. It's a saga of human spirit and talent, of dreams and determination, of spectacular victories and heartfelt moments.

So, are you ready? Do you have your baseball cap adjusted and your glove on hand? Do you feel the thrill of anticipation? Can you hear the roar of the crowd in your ears? Good! You're all set to dive into the world of baseball, a world where every moment is an opportunity for something amazing to happen.

As we step onto the field, we invite you to experience the magic of baseball through the stories in this book. Join us as we explore the grand game of baseball, reliving its most amazing moments, celebrating its heroes, and understanding why it has captured the hearts of millions around the world.

Let's step up to the plate, and let's play ball!

# Chapter One:

# Babe Ruth's Called Shot: A Tale of Confidence

Once upon a time, in a bustling city known as Chicago, a baseball legend named Babe Ruth stepped up to the plate. The date was October 1, 1932, and the excitement was bubbling in the air as Ruth's New York Yankees were playing the Chicago Cubs in Game 3 of the World Series.

The World Series was like the Olympics of baseball, where the two best teams faced off to determine who was the ultimate champion. Babe Ruth, also known as the 'Sultan of Swat,' was already a superstar, famous for his powerful hits and larger-than-life personality. He had a talent for hitting the baseball out of the park, which is called a home run. These home runs often changed the course of a game, making him a hero in the eyes of his fans.

But let's back up a bit. Who was this man they called Babe Ruth?

George Herman Ruth Jr., or Babe Ruth, as we know him, was born in Baltimore, Maryland, in 1895. As a young boy, he was always full of energy, and his love for baseball was evident from the start. He started his career as a pitcher, but his exceptional talent for hitting home runs led him to become an outfielder. The more home runs he hit, the more fans flocked to see him play. And believe me, he hit a lot of them!

Now, back to that exciting day in Chicago. The stadium was filled with anticipation. The crowd was a sea of faces, some cheering for the Yankees, some for the Cubs. The noise was deafening as Babe Ruth walked towards the plate, his bat swinging casually in his hand. He had a powerful presence, and all eyes were on him.

Ruth was already having a great game. He had hit a home run earlier, and now he was back for more. But the Cubs fans were teasing and booing him. Some say that even the Cubs players were joining in. But Babe Ruth, ever the showman, wasn't going to be put off by a bit of teasing.

Standing there at the plate, Ruth did something that surprised everyone. He held out one finger, pointing towards the centerfield stands, far, far away. Then he confidently readied himself for the next pitch.

Why was he pointing, you ask? Well, dear readers, Babe Ruth was not just indicating where he intended to hit the ball. He was promising it.

Charlie Root, the pitcher for the Cubs, wound up and delivered his throw. It zoomed through the air towards Ruth. With a powerful swing, Ruth connected with the ball. And the next moment? The ball was soaring high and far, flying straight towards the spot Ruth had pointed to.

The crowd went silent for a moment, watching in disbelief as the ball continued its flight, and then... it disappeared over the centerfield wall, exactly where Ruth had pointed!

The stadium erupted in cheers and shouts. People were hugging and laughing, and some were even crying. Babe Ruth had done the impossible! He had called his shot, promising to hit a home run and then doing just that. It was a display of such audacity and confidence that it's still talked about to this day.

That called shot showed what Babe Ruth was made of. He was a player who wasn't afraid to dream big, to take risks, and to put his all into every single game. He loved baseball, he loved his fans, and he knew how to put on a show.

This tale teaches us something valuable. It's not just about baseball. It's about believing in yourself and having the confidence to follow through with your goals, even when others doubt you. Babe Ruth showed us that with courage and a dash of flair, you can leave a mark on the world that people will remember forever.

In the games that followed, Ruth continued to display his prowess. Even after the famous 'called shot', he never let the pressure get to him. He simply kept on playing the game he loved with the confidence that had made him a star.

And it was this confidence that had led Ruth from the streets of Baltimore to the heights of the baseball world. His beginnings were humble, but his dreams were big, as big as the home runs he used to smash out of the ballpark.

Young Babe Ruth hadn't had it easy. Growing up in a poor neighborhood with seven siblings, life was a struggle. He was sent to St. Mary's Industrial School for Boys, a school for orphans and troubled children, when he was only seven. But it was at St. Mary's that Ruth discovered his love for baseball.

The boys would play baseball every chance they got, and Ruth was the star of the show, even then. He would hit the ball so far that the others would stand and watch in amazement. The more he played, the better he got, and it wasn't long before his talent caught the eye of a Baltimore Orioles scout.

At just 19 years old, Babe Ruth began his professional baseball career. But the road to stardom was not smooth. Ruth had to work hard, practicing day in and day out. He was determined to be the best, and nothing was going to stand in his way.

And he did become the best. Ruth went on to play for 22 seasons, smashing record after record. His called shot in the 1932 World Series was just one of the many unforgettable moments in his career.

But Ruth's impact on the game went beyond the baseball field. He was a larger-than-life character who changed the way people thought about sports. He showed that baseball was not just about winning or losing, but about the thrill of the game, the shared excitement of the fans, and the sheer joy of playing.

Ruth's confidence was contagious. He showed his fans that it was okay to dream big, to aim high, and to have fun while doing it. His audacious called shot was not just about hitting a home run; it was a message to everyone watching that you could achieve great things if you believe in yourself.

But Ruth was not just a confident player; he was also a generous person off the field. He never forgot where he came from and would often visit hospitals, orphanages, and schools, offering words of encouragement and sharing his love for the game with children who dreamed of following in his footsteps.

In the end, Babe Ruth's tale is not just a story about a baseball player. It's a story about a boy who believed in himself and, with confidence and determination, became a legend.

As we learn about Babe Ruth and his incredible called shot, let's remember that we all have a little bit of the Sultan of Swat in us. We can face challenges head-on, dream big, and, with a bit of confidence, maybe even call our shots in life. Because, in the end, it's not about whether you win or lose, but how you play the game.

And that's the end of our first chapter, kids. But don't go anywhere, because there's a lot more baseball history to explore. As we turn the page, we'll discover more amazing stories, just like Babe Ruth's, that will remind us to dream big, play fair, and always believe in ourselves. So stay tuned, and keep your baseball cap on, because this journey through the most amazing baseball stories of all time is just getting started!

# Chapter Two:
# Jackie Robinson Breaks the Color Barrier: A Story of Bravery

In our first chapter, we explored the life and legacy of Babe Ruth, a baseball legend whose audacious confidence and record-breaking performances earned him a place in history. But sometimes, a player becomes a hero not just for their statistics or spectacular plays, but for their courage off the field, for their determination to challenge the status quo, and for their resilience in the face of adversity. Such is the story of Jackie Robinson, a man whose bravery changed not only baseball but also the course of American history.

Born in 1919, in Cairo, Georgia, Jack Roosevelt Robinson, known to us as Jackie, was the youngest of five children. His parents were sharecroppers, and Jackie grew up in a time when racial segregation was the law of the land. But the hardships he encountered early in life did not deter him; rather, they fueled his determination to succeed.

Robinson's athletic abilities became evident in his high school years, where he excelled in various sports, including football, basketball, track, and baseball. His exceptional skill and prowess on the field earned him a scholarship to the University of California, Los Angeles (UCLA), where he became the first student to win varsity letters in four sports.

Jackie's journey towards breaking baseball's color barrier, however, began earnestly after his service in the U.S. Army during World War II. Upon leaving the army, Robinson played for the Kansas City Monarchs, a team in the Negro Leagues, the professional baseball leagues that housed African American players barred from Major League Baseball.

In 1945, a man named Branch Rickey, the president of the Brooklyn Dodgers, decided to challenge the unwritten rule that excluded African American players from Major League Baseball. Rickey knew that to accomplish this, he needed a player who was immensely talented and possessed an unshakeable spirit, someone who could withstand the inevitable backlash that would arise from breaking the color barrier. Jackie Robinson was that player.

When Robinson accepted Rickey's offer to play for the Dodgers, he knew the journey ahead would be challenging. He would face hostility, discrimination, and even threats. Yet, he chose to step forward, understanding the significance of what his presence on the field would represent.

In his first season with the Dodgers in 1947, Robinson faced adversity with courage and dignity. Despite receiving hate mail, hearing jeers from spectators, and experiencing animosity from fellow players, Robinson remained focused on the game. His performance was so stellar he earned the title of Rookie of the Year.

Yet, Robinson's influence transcended his baseball stats. By breaking the color barrier, he challenged the deeply ingrained racial prejudices of his time. His presence on the field symbolized the beginning of integration in baseball, serving as a beacon of hope for equality in a time of rampant racial discrimination.

Even after his retirement from the sport in 1956, Robinson continued to advocate for racial equality. He used his fame to challenge racial prejudices and worked tirelessly to ensure that opportunities were extended to African Americans in all spheres of life.

Robinson's life was a testament to the power of resilience, courage, and determination. He faced adversities that would have discouraged many, but he remained undeterred, standing firm in his conviction for equality. His legacy continues to inspire many around the world, reinforcing the belief that with bravery and perseverance, barriers can be broken, and change is possible.

In 1997, Major League Baseball universally retired Robinson's number, 42, across all teams - a first in the history of the sport. This was an acknowledgment of Robinson's significant impact on baseball and a tribute to his courage and perseverance. Today, every year on April 15th, known as Jackie Robinson Day, players across the league honor Jackie's legacy by wearing the number 42, serving as a strong reminder of the strides made in the realm of equality and the work still ahead.

Though Jackie Robinson left us in 1972, his story continues to inspire generations. He was not only a phenomenal athlete but also a man of unyielding courage and unwavering determination. His willingness to take a stand, to endure immense pressure, and to rise above it all is a testament to his extraordinary character.

Let's take a closer look at some of the challenges Robinson faced and how he triumphed over them. On his first day with the Dodgers, he stepped onto a field filled with thousands of spectators – many of them were openly hostile, simply because of the color of his skin. There were teammates who refused to play with him and opponents who targeted him. Yet, Jackie held his head high. He refused to let their prejudice define him.

Robinson was a natural on the baseball field. He had a batting average of .311 over ten seasons, an impressive feat for any player. But his impact was not just in the runs he scored or the bases he stole. It was in the way he carried himself, the way he tackled adversity, and the way he never let hatred and bias break his spirit.

One cannot discuss Jackie Robinson without speaking about the 1947 season. Despite the hostility he faced, Robinson shone on the field. He was named the National League Rookie of the Year, an acknowledgment of his remarkable performance and talent.

But, perhaps more importantly, his success that season was a slap in the face of the prejudice and bias that had tried to undermine him.

Jackie's influence and impact did not stop when he hung up his cleats. After his retirement from baseball, Robinson continued to break barriers and push for equality. He became the first African American television analyst in Major League Baseball and the first African American vice president of a major American corporation, Chock full o'Nuts.

Moreover, Jackie used his platform to advance the civil rights movement. He understood the value of his voice and his influence, and he did not shy away from speaking up against discrimination and advocating for change. Robinson was a role model, a trailblazer, and a tireless advocate for racial equality.

Beyond his significant contributions to sports and society, Jackie Robinson was also a family man. In 1946, he married Rachel Annetta Isum, a nursing student he had met at UCLA. They had three children together - Jackie Jr., Sharon, and David. Rachel provided immense support for Jackie, standing by his side through all the trials and tribulations, reinforcing his strength and resolve.

Off the field, Jackie was known to be as fierce and determined as he was on it. He often advocated for civil rights and actively participated in events aimed at promoting racial equality. After retiring from baseball, he became increasingly active in the civil rights movement, joining forces with iconic figures like Martin Luther King Jr. and Malcom X.

In 1964, Jackie co-founded the Freedom National Bank, a commercial bank owned by African Americans, serving as its first Chairman of the Board. His intent was to provide economic opportunities to those who had been denied them. This endeavor reflected his lifelong commitment to equality and social justice.

Despite the fame and recognition, Robinson never forgot his roots. He used his influence to draw attention to the issues that mattered to him - equality, justice, and opportunity for all. He once famously said, "A life is not important except in the impact it has on other lives." By this measure, Robinson's life was incredibly important.

In the later years of his life, Jackie also faced personal tragedy. His eldest son, Jackie Jr., struggled with drug addiction, a battle he unfortunately lost in a car accident in 1971. This tragedy led Jackie and Rachel to start the Jackie Robinson Foundation, which provides scholarships and mentoring for college students of color. Even in his grief, Jackie found a way to create a legacy of hope and opportunity.

Jackie Robinson passed away in 1972, but his impact remains palpable. Each year on April 15, every player in Major League Baseball wears the number 42 in his honor. It's a visible reminder of the man who broke the color barrier and changed the course of history. The legacy of Jackie Robinson extends far beyond the baseball field. It is woven into the fabric of American history.

In recognition of his immense contributions to both sports and society, Jackie Robinson was posthumously awarded the

Presidential Medal of Freedom, the highest civilian award in the United States, by President Ronald Reagan in 1984.

The story of Jackie Robinson is one that should be remembered and celebrated. It's a story about challenging norms, overcoming adversity, and standing up for what is right. It's a story that reminds us that the path to change is often filled with obstacles, but with courage, determination, and resilience, those obstacles can be overcome.

As we move on to the next chapter of our book, let's carry with us the lessons from Jackie Robinson's life. He showed us the importance of standing up for what is right, even when it's hard. He demonstrated that change is possible if we have the courage to fight for it. And he taught us that no barrier is too high if we're willing to reach for the stars.

# Chapter Three:

# The Miracle Mets: An Underdog Triumph

In the history of baseball, few stories are as inspirational and captivating as that of the 1969 New York Mets, affectionately referred to as "The Miracle Mets". It's a story that reaffirms the belief that with determination, grit, and a little bit of faith, even the most unlikely underdogs can triumph.

The New York Mets, established in 1962, had a less than stellar start to their journey in Major League Baseball. In their inaugural season, they racked up 120 losses, a record for the most losses in a single season since 1899. For the first seven seasons, the team never managed to climb out of the last place in the National League standings. It seemed that the Mets were destined to remain at the bottom, forever playing second fiddle to their cross-town rivals, the mighty New York Yankees.

However, everything began to change in 1968 when Gil Hodges was brought in to manage the team. Hodges, a former All-Star first baseman, brought a new sense of discipline, focus, and confidence to the struggling team. He started by instilling in the players a belief that they could win, despite their previous record. He nurtured a culture of teamwork and resilience, qualities that would play a vital role in the miraculous season to come.

As the 1969 season began, few could have predicted the transformation that awaited the Mets. They kicked off the season with their usual run of inconsistent performances, but something felt different. The players showed a new sense of determination and a newfound belief in themselves. This became more evident as the season progressed. The Mets began to play better, winning more games, and gradually climbing up the National League standings.

A significant contributor to their success was a strong pitching roster, which included future Hall of Famers Tom Seaver and Nolan Ryan. Seaver, also known as "Tom Terrific," was the ace of the team. His stellar performance throughout the season, which included a league-leading 25 wins, earned him the Cy Young Award.

Nolan Ryan, though still early in his career, showed signs of the formidable pitcher he would become. Other players, like Jerry Koosman and Gary Gentry, also made significant contributions to the team's strong pitching game.

On the offensive side, the team lacked big hitters but made up for it with their spirit and tenacity. Players like Cleon Jones, Art Shamsky, and Ron Swoboda may not have been household names, but their determination, combined with timely hitting, played a crucial role in the Mets' success.

By the end of the season, the Mets had won a staggering 100 games, a far cry from their previous losing seasons. They clinched the National League East Division title, securing their place in the playoffs for the first time. However, the most challenging tests were yet to come.

In the National League Championship Series, the Mets faced the Atlanta Braves, featuring the legendary Hank Aaron. The Braves were considered favorites, but the Mets defied expectations. They swept the Braves in three straight games, showcasing their dominant pitching and timely hitting. Their victory in the NLCS earned them a ticket to the World Series, where they would face the heavily favored Baltimore Orioles.

The Orioles, boasting a line-up of six All-Stars and three twenty-game winners in their pitching staff, were considered by many to be one of the greatest teams of all time. On paper, they outmatched the Mets in almost every way. Yet, the underdog Mets were undeterred. They carried the same resilience and determination that had powered their journey so far into the World Series.

The World Series began on October 11, 1969. The Mets faced the Orioles at Baltimore's Memorial Stadium. The first game did not go in favor of the Mets. Despite a good start, the Mets lost 4-1, giving the Orioles an early lead in the series. It seemed the critics might be right - maybe the Mets were outmatched after all. But, as we've seen, these were not the same old Mets. They remained undeterred.

In Game 2, Jerry Koosman took to the mound for the Mets. Koosman had been a crucial part of the Mets' pitching arsenal throughout the season, and that day, he pitched a phenomenal game. Despite the Orioles taking an early lead, the Mets rallied back and won the game 2-1. The underdogs had struck back, tying the series.

As the series moved to New York for Game 3, the Mets found their rhythm. Gary Gentry, a rookie, was the starting pitcher, and he threw a gem of a game. With some timely hitting and a surprise relief appearance by Nolan Ryan, the Mets took the game 5-0, stunning the Orioles and the baseball world.

Game 4 again saw the resilient Mets rally late in the game to secure a 2-1 victory, taking a 3-1 lead in the series. The Mets were one win away from completing their miraculous journey. The atmosphere was electric as they entered Game 5.

On October 16, 1969, in front of a packed Shea Stadium, the Mets took the field. The game was tight, with both teams showcasing their skills. However, the Mets pulled ahead, eventually winning the game 5-3 and clinching the World Series.

In a season where they had been pegged as 100-1 long shots to win the championship, the New York Mets had defied the odds. They had gone from perennial losers to World Series champions in a span of seven short years. It was truly a miracle.

As we reflect on the story of the Miracle Mets, we learn the power of resilience, the importance of belief, and the magic of teamwork. It shows us that even when the odds are stacked against us, even when the critics doubt us, and even when we have a history of falling short, we can still triumph.

In the chapters to come, we'll delve into more such amazing stories from the world of baseball. We'll meet more inspiring individuals, learn from their journeys, and celebrate their victories. But, for now, let's bask in the glow of the Miracle Mets' triumph and the lessons it offers us.

The Mets' victory lap around Shea Stadium that October evening wasn't just a celebration of their win; it was a celebration of the human spirit, of the fight against the odds, and of the dreams that we dare to dream.

As we close the chapter on the Miracle Mets, we can take away some profound lessons. Let's revisit a few of the key moments and extract the invaluable life lessons that they impart.

The team's transformation under manager Gil Hodges underscores the importance of leadership. Hodges believed in his team and helped the players believe in themselves. He instilled a culture of discipline, resilience, and teamwork, which served as the foundation for the team's success. This teaches us the power of positive reinforcement and the importance of fostering an environment that encourages growth and confidence.

The perseverance shown by the players is another remarkable aspect of the Miracle Mets' journey. Despite their less than stellar past performance and the numerous challenges they faced, the Mets never gave up. They continued to strive for improvement, to learn from their mistakes, and to move forward. The team's perseverance teaches us to never lose hope, to remain dedicated, and to continually strive for improvement, no matter the circumstances.

The unity displayed by the team is another crucial lesson. Baseball, like many other sports, is a team game. The success of a team hinges on the coordinated efforts of all its players. The Mets' story is a testament to the power of teamwork. Each player, from the pitchers to the fielders, contributed to the team's success. Their story teaches us that while individual skills are important, the success of a team lies in its ability to work together towards a common goal.

The Miracle Mets were not a team of superstar players. They didn't have the most powerful hitters or the most dominant pitchers. What they had was a group of players who played to their strengths, who believed in each other, and who never gave up. They had players who rose to the occasion when it mattered most, displaying the qualities of true sportsmanship. Their story highlights the fact that you don't always need to have the best players to win; you need players who play their best when it counts the most.

And finally, the story of the Miracle Mets teaches us about the beauty of sports. Sports have the power to inspire, to uplift, and to unite. The Mets' journey from the bottom of the league to World Series champions captured the imagination of people around the world. It served as a beacon of hope, illustrating that with dedication, perseverance, and teamwork, anything is possible.

In the next chapter, we'll dive into the exciting home run race of 1998 between Mark McGwire and Sammy Sosa. It's a story filled with suspense, competition, and remarkable achievements. But until then, let's carry forward the lessons we've learned from the Miracle Mets.

Remember, in life, as in baseball, the game isn't over until the last out. So, keep playing, keep striving, and keep believing in the miracle of your potential.

# Chapter Four:

# The Great Home Run Race of '98:

# McGwire vs. Sosa

Baseball is a sport that's been filled with thrilling moments and unforgettable events. But few have captured the nation's imagination quite like the home run race of 1998 between Mark McGwire of the St. Louis Cardinals and Sammy Sosa of the Chicago Cubs. This chapter brings you the roller-coaster ride of this legendary competition, which turned into a summer-long spectacle that transcended baseball.

In the late 1990s, Major League Baseball was recovering from the damaging 1994-95 strike that had led to the cancellation of the World Series for the first time since 1904. Fans were disillusioned, and the sport was in desperate need of a captivating story to reignite the love for the game. As if on cue, the 1998 season brought just that – a head-to-head race between two exceptional athletes, a competition that enthralled not only America but the whole world.

The record in question was the single-season home run record of 61, set by the New York Yankees' Roger Maris in 1961. Maris's record had stood unchallenged for 37 years, and although several players had come close, none had been able to surpass it. Then, in 1998, Mark McGwire and Sammy Sosa embarked on a season-long pursuit of this hallowed record, and baseball fans were treated to one of the most exciting home run races in history.

Mark McGwire, a first baseman for the St. Louis Cardinals, was a seasoned slugger who had already built a reputation as a powerful hitter. Standing at a towering 6 feet 5 inches and built like a freight train, McGwire was an imposing figure at the plate. Known for his ferocious swing, he had the ability to send balls soaring over the fence with seeming ease.

Sammy Sosa, a right fielder for the Chicago Cubs, contrasted McGwire in many ways. While he wasn't as physically imposing as McGwire, Sosa was known for his quick and compact swing, along with his charisma and enthusiastic playing style. His infectious smile and signature 'hop' after hitting a home run endeared him to fans.

As the 1998 season got underway, both players began racking up home runs at an impressive pace. But it wasn't until June that the home run race truly caught fire. Sosa hit an astonishing 20 home runs that month, a record in itself, and by the end of June, both players were on track to challenge Maris's record. The nation was captivated, and every at-bat by McGwire and Sosa became a must-watch event.

As the season rolled into July, the excitement surrounding the home run race escalated. The media coverage was intense, with every game, every at-bat, and every home run attracting national attention. Both players seemed to thrive under the spotlight, consistently delivering jaw-dropping performances.

In August, the race tightened even further. By this time, McGwire and Sosa were neck and neck in their quest for 62. On September 8, 1998, in front of a packed home crowd at Busch Stadium in St. Louis, McGwire did the unthinkable. In the fourth inning, he smashed a pitch from the Chicago Cubs' Steve Trachsel over the left-field wall for his 62nd home run, breaking Maris's longstanding record. As the ball cleared the fence, the crowd erupted in deafening cheers, and his teammates swarmed him at home plate in a scene of jubilation.

But the race was far from over. Sosa, ever the gracious competitor, was one of the first to congratulate McGwire. But he didn't let McGwire's achievement slow him down. Just a few days later, Sosa also surpassed Maris's record, hitting his 62nd home run on September 13.

The race for the record had turned into a race for the ages. McGwire and Sosa continued to blast home runs, pushing each other and the record to new heights. By the end of the season, McGwire finished with an astonishing 70 home runs, setting a new single-season record. Sosa wasn't far behind, concluding his remarkable season with 66 home runs.

The home run race of '98 had successfully captured the imagination of the public and revitalized the nation's love for baseball. It was more than just a contest between two extraordinary athletes; it was a celebration of the game's most electrifying play—the home run. The excitement, suspense, and friendly competition between McGwire and Sosa reminded everyone of the joy, thrill, and camaraderie that are at the heart of baseball.

Looking back, we can learn many valuable lessons from this legendary home run race. It's a testament to healthy competition and sportsmanship. Even as they chased the same goal, McGwire and Sosa showed great respect and admiration for each other. Their camaraderie serves as a reminder that while sports are competitive, they should also bring people together.

Furthermore, the race underscores the importance of perseverance and hard work. Both players had put in countless hours of practice and conditioning to develop their skills. Their journey reminds us that achieving greatness requires dedication, discipline, and a relentless desire to improve.

Finally, the home run race of '98 is a shining example of how sports can inspire and unite people. Amid all the excitement and spectacle, we find a deeper truth: that sports have the power to bring us together, to inspire us, and to give us something to cheer for, irrespective of our differences.

The home run race of 1998 was not only a test of physical prowess but also of mental fortitude. The intense media attention and the weight of a historic record created an environment of immense stress. Yet, both McGwire and Sosa managed to maintain their focus throughout the season, demonstrating their mental strength.

However, it is also important to note that the accomplishments of both players have been clouded by allegations of performance-enhancing drug use. In the years following the home run race, both McGwire and Sosa faced accusations that they had used steroids during their careers. These allegations have raised questions about the legitimacy of their achievements and have sparked broader discussions about the use of performance-enhancing drugs in sports.

Despite these controversies, there's no denying that the race brought much-needed positivity and unity to the baseball community. The shared excitement of the competition served as a unifying force for fans around the world, underlining the power of sports to bring people together.

Also worth mentioning are the teams and individuals who supported McGwire and Sosa throughout this journey. The coaches, trainers, and support staff who worked tirelessly behind the scenes played a crucial role in their success.

The fans, too, played a vital role. The cheers that greeted each home run, the signs of support in the stands, and the countless people watching at home - their passion and support were integral to the race.

The 1998 home run race also taught important lessons about handling pressure. Despite the intense scrutiny and the magnitude of their feats, both McGwire and Sosa showed an ability to stay focused on the task at hand, a lesson that can be applied in all aspects of life.

The story of the 1998 home run race is also a celebration of baseball. Despite the controversy surrounding it, the tale of this race underscores the drama, the anticipation, the shared excitement, and the unforgettable moments that the sport provides.

As we wrap up this chapter on the home run race between Mark McGwire and Sammy Sosa, we hope you've enjoyed the ride and taken away some valuable lessons. Even though their achievements have been tainted by controversy, the thrill and unity that their competition brought to the sport of baseball remain a memorable part of its history. As we turn the page, we'll explore another remarkable story from the world of baseball - the perfect game pitched by Don Larsen in the World Series, a tale that perfectly encapsulates the unpredictability and sheer joy of this beautiful game.

# Chapter Five:

# The Perfect Game: Don Larsen's World Series

It was October 8, 1956. Game 5 of the World Series was about to begin at Yankee Stadium. The New York Yankees were facing the Brooklyn Dodgers in a fierce battle for the title. The Series was tied at 2 games each, and for this game, the Yankees had entrusted their fate to a relatively unknown pitcher - Don Larsen.

Don Larsen, a tall, quiet man from Michigan, wasn't considered a star in the baseball world. In fact, just a year before, he had a less than impressive season, losing more games than he won. However, on this fateful day, Larsen was given a chance to show his worth on the grandest stage in baseball.

The game began under clear skies with a sense of anticipation and excitement in the air. Little did the crowd know, they were about to witness one of the most extraordinary feats in baseball history.

Larsen's performance started off solidly. He was focused, calm, and, most importantly, effective. He retired the first few batters he faced with relative ease. The Dodgers, known for their formidable lineup, couldn't seem to figure Larsen out. His pitches were accurate and fast, and he was masterfully mixing them up, keeping the Dodgers' hitters off-balance.

As the game progressed, so did Larsen's performance. Inning after inning, he continued to retire the Dodgers' batters. Some went down on strikes, others grounded out or popped out, but none could manage a hit. As Larsen walked off the mound after the end of the 6th inning, he had a realization - he hadn't allowed a single hit. He was, unintentionally, on his way to pitching a perfect game.

As Larsen returned to the mound for the seventh inning, a sense of anticipation hung heavy in the air. Some in the crowd had started to notice what was happening. A perfect game in baseball is a rare feat, but a perfect game in a World Series was unheard of.

Despite this growing pressure, Larsen remained composed. He stayed focused on his task: getting the batters out, one by one. He kept his pitches precise and fast, continuing to puzzle the Dodgers' batters. The seventh inning came and went, and still, not a single Dodger had reached base.

In the dugout, Larsen's teammates noticed what was happening, but none of them mentioned it. In baseball, there's a superstition that you never talk about a perfect game or no-hitter while it's in progress. The belief is that it could jinx the outcome. So, despite the mounting tension and excitement, they all kept silent about the unfolding drama.

The eighth inning was more of the same. Larsen was untouchable. His command over his pitches was unwavering. As he walked off the mound after retiring the side, he was just three outs away from achieving the unthinkable.

Then came the ninth and final inning. The crowd was on the edge of their seats. The atmosphere was electric with a mix of nervous anticipation and excitement. As Larsen walked onto the mound, he could feel the weight of the moment. But he also knew he was just three outs away from making history.

Facing Larsen in the ninth inning were some of the toughest hitters in the Dodgers' lineup. But Larsen was not to be denied. With the same composure he had shown all game, he got the first two batters out. The crowd held its collective breath. One more out, and Larsen would have achieved perfection.

The last batter Larsen had to face was Dale Mitchell, a seasoned player known for his skill at making contact with the ball. The air was thick with tension as Mitchell stepped up to the plate. Larsen took a deep breath, focused his gaze, and delivered his pitch. Mitchell swung - and missed. Strike one. Larsen wound up again and delivered another strike. The crowd was on its feet. Just one more strike, and the perfect game would be complete.

Larsen wound up one more time and delivered his pitch. Mitchell swung and missed again. The crowd erupted into cheers. Don Larsen had just pitched the first - and, as of my knowledge cutoff in September 2021, still the only - perfect game in World Series history. He had faced 27 batters and not one had reached base. It was, indeed, a perfect game.

The significance of this feat cannot be overstated. In the long history of Major League Baseball, there have only been a handful of perfect games. But to do it in a World Series, under the intense pressure and scrutiny that comes with it, is something else entirely. It is a testament to Larsen's focus, skill, and resilience.

In the grand scheme of his career, Don Larsen was not a superstar. He wasn't the most consistent pitcher, nor did he have a long list of accolades. But on that October day in 1956, he was perfect. His achievement serves as a reminder that greatness can come from the most unexpected places, and that with determination and focus, anything is possible.

Despite the whirlwind of celebration and congratulations that followed, Larsen remained humble. As he later reflected on the game, he admitted, "I had no idea I was pitching a perfect game. I didn't even know until after the game when all the reporters came up to me."

What's more, he also emphasized the team effort behind his individual success. He credited his catcher, Yogi Berra, for expertly guiding him through the game, the defense for backing him up on every play, and the entire team for their support and belief in him. Even in the spotlight, Larsen never lost sight of the fact that baseball is a team sport.

From this unforgettable game, there are many lessons we can learn. One is the importance of focus and perseverance. Despite his previous season's struggles, Larsen didn't give up. He kept working, kept improving, and when the moment came, he was ready.

Another lesson is about dealing with pressure. In one of the highest-stakes scenarios in baseball, Larsen kept his cool. He didn't let the gravity of the situation overwhelm him. Instead, he stayed focused on the task at hand: each pitch, each batter.

And perhaps the most important lesson is about the unpredictability and magic of baseball itself. Before that day, no one would have guessed that Don Larsen, an average pitcher by most accounts, would pitch a perfect game in the World Series. But that's the beauty of the sport. On any given day, anyone can be a hero. That's a message we can all take to heart, no matter what field we're playing on.

As we look back on this extraordinary moment in baseball history, it's clear that Don Larsen's perfect game was more than just a masterful performance on the field. It was a demonstration of focus, determination, teamwork, and humility. It's a story that reminds us of the power of self-belief and the magic of baseball.

# Chapter Six:

# Say Hey! Willie Mays and the Catch of the Century

The year was 1954, and the World Series was in full swing. On one side was the Cleveland Indians, who had boasted an impressive record that season and were the favorites to win. On the other side was the New York Giants, underdogs, yes, but with a secret weapon of their own. A young, dynamic center fielder by the name of Willie Mays.

Born in Alabama in 1931, Willie Mays grew up in a world where baseball was a way of life. He played the game with a joy and a flair that would eventually earn him the nickname, 'The Say Hey Kid.' By 1954, at the age of just 23, Mays had already made a name for himself as one of the most exciting players in baseball.

It was September 29th, a sunny day at the Polo Grounds in New York City, and the stage was set for Game 1 of the World Series. The Giants had managed to hold their own against the mighty Indians, and as the game entered the top of the 8th inning, the score was tied 2-2.

With two men on base, the Indians' power-hitting first baseman Vic Wertz was at the plate. Wertz had already had a successful day, having hit a triple and a double earlier in the game. Now, he was ready to make his mark again.

On the mound for the Giants was reliever Don Liddle. With the count at two balls and one strike, Liddle wound up and delivered the pitch. Wertz swung and connected solidly. The ball rocketed into the air, soaring high and deep towards center field. The crowd held its breath.

Willie Mays, positioned over 400 feet away in center field, took off in a sprint. With his back to the infield, he raced towards the spot where he believed the ball was going to land. This was a massive outfield, and the ball was going deep, well over 450 feet from home plate. It seemed an impossible catch to make.

As Mays sprinted towards the warning track, he stole a quick glance over his shoulder. He knew he was close, but would he be close enough? With the crowd watching with bated breath, Mays reached the warning track, signifying he was just a step away from the outfield wall. He glanced once more over his shoulder, reached up, and—miraculously—the ball fell into his glove just as he hit the warning track. In one fluid motion, he stopped, whirled around, and threw the ball back towards the infield, holding the runners on their bases.

The crowd erupted. Players in the dugout leapt to their feet. Everyone in the stadium, and many more listening on radios or watching on black and white televisions across the country, knew they had just witnessed something extraordinary.

The play would forever be known as 'The Catch.' It was a moment that would be replayed countless times in the years to come, a shining example of athletic brilliance, keen judgment, and raw speed. Some say it was the greatest defensive play in the history of baseball. Mays, however, shrugged it off with typical modesty. "I don't think it was such a big deal," he would later say. "When I hit the ball, I want it to stay hit. But when the other guy hits the ball, I want to catch it."

The Giants would go on to win that game in the 10th inning, and eventually sweep the Indians in the series to become World Series champions. Willie Mays would continue to have an illustrious career, known as much for his spectacular defense as for his powerful hitting. He played with joy, with flair, and with a boyish love for the game that would endear him to fans for generations.

The real magic of 'The Catch,' though, is not just in the physical act itself - impressive as that was. The real magic lies in what it represents. In that one moment, Willie Mays showed us what it means to never give up, to stretch ourselves to our limits, and to always believe in the possibility of the extraordinary.

Mays, with his trademark cap flying off, sprinting with abandon, his back to the infield, wasn't just making a play. He was defying expectations, shattering limitations, and showing a young, post-war generation that anything - absolutely anything - was possible if you were willing to go the distance.

It's important to remember, too, that Mays wasn't born a superstar. As a young boy in the Jim Crow South, he faced obstacles that would have derailed many. He honed his skills in the Negro Leagues before the color barrier was broken. His first season in the Major Leagues was a struggle, and he considered quitting before a pep talk from his manager, Leo Durocher, convinced him to persist.

But Mays stayed the course. He worked hard, remained true to his love for the game, and became one of the greatest players in the history of baseball. Along the way, he inspired countless others with his enduring humility, his joyful spirit, and his never-say-die attitude.

"The Catch" was not just a pivotal moment in a World Series game. It was a symbol of Mays's entire approach to life and to baseball. It was a testament to his commitment, his dedication, and his belief in doing the impossible.

Today, the story of Willie Mays and 'The Catch' serves as an inspiration not only to young athletes but to anyone who dreams of achieving great things. It's a story that transcends the world of baseball and touches the hearts of people from all walks of life.

The true legacy of Willie Mays, however, extends far beyond 'The Catch'. His phenomenal career statistics speak for themselves, but what really set Mays apart was the way he played the game. His boundless energy, his joy, and his love for baseball were infectious. He played with a childlike enthusiasm that was utterly captivating, earning him legions of fans across the country.

Off the field, Mays was equally impressive. Despite the challenges and pressures he faced as one of the few Black players in the Major Leagues at the time, he always carried himself with grace and dignity. He became a role model for millions, breaking down racial barriers and paving the way for future generations of players.

In many ways, Willie Mays represents the very best of baseball. He embodied the spirit of the game, the excitement, the joy, and the sheer love of play. And through his remarkable career, he showed us all what can be achieved when talent is combined with hard work, determination, and a never-give-up attitude.

In Willie Mays' story, there are lessons for us all. We learn about the power of perseverance and the importance of never giving up. We learn that, with hard work and determination, we can defy expectations and accomplish extraordinary things. And we learn that no matter how high the ball is hit, no matter how far the fence may seem, there's always a chance to make the catch if we're willing to give it our all.

# Chapter Seven:

# Kirk Gibson's Impossible Homerun: A Tale of Perseverance

It was the bottom of the ninth inning in Game One of the 1988 World Series. The Los Angeles Dodgers were trailing the Oakland Athletics by one run. Dodgers Stadium was buzzing with anticipation, hope, and anxiety. Fans held their breath as they watched Kirk Gibson, one of the Dodgers' star players, struggle to the plate.

Kirk Gibson was an athletic dynamo, a former college football star turned baseball powerhouse. His competitive spirit was legendary, and his ability to deliver in clutch situations had made him an invaluable asset to the Dodgers' team. But as he limped up to the plate, his grimace unmistakable, the odds seemed stacked against him.

Just days before, Gibson had injured both legs. His left hamstring was strained, and his right knee was sprained. He was in considerable pain and had spent most of the game in the trainer's room, watching his teammates on a television screen. But when his team needed him the most, Gibson refused to stay benched.

But before we learn the rest of the story, to fully appreciate the magnitude of what Kirk Gibson was about to do, it's important to understand the man himself and his journey leading up to this monumental moment.

Kirk Gibson was born in Michigan in 1957 and was a gifted athlete from a young age. He excelled in football and baseball, and his natural talent combined with an unyielding work ethic. In college, Gibson was a wide receiver for the Michigan State Spartans football team, and his athleticism shone brightly on the gridiron. His potential was such that he was selected by the St. Louis Cardinals in the 7th round of the 1979 NFL Draft. But baseball was Gibson's true love, and he chose the diamond over the gridiron. He was drafted by the Detroit Tigers in the 1st round of the 1978 MLB Draft.

As a young player in Detroit, Gibson quickly established himself as a force to be reckoned with. His combination of power and speed made him a standout player, and his fearless style of play won him fans and the respect of his peers. He was an integral part of the Tigers' 1984 World Series Championship team. His years in Detroit were marked by notable achievements, but Gibson was only getting started.

After the 1987 season, Gibson joined the Los Angeles Dodgers as a free agent. Under the guidance of legendary manager Tommy Lasorda, Gibson's star shone brighter than ever. He had a fantastic season in 1988, hitting .290 with 25 home runs and 76 RBIs, earning him the National League MVP award.

But as successful as the regular season was, the postseason was shaping up to be a monumental challenge. Gibson's injuries were severe, and it seemed unlikely he would be able to contribute much to the Dodgers' World Series efforts. As Game One approached, the question on everyone's mind was, "Will Gibson be able to play?"

Despite his painful injuries, Gibson was determined to make a difference for his team. He knew the odds were against him. He couldn't run without pain, and every swing of the bat was a challenge. But Gibson was not the type of player to back down from a challenge. He was a competitor to his core, and he was ready to give everything he had for his team.

His grit and determination set the stage for one of the most dramatic moments in World Series history, a moment that would become a symbol of perseverance and determination.

The day of Game One arrived. Gibson was not in the starting lineup due to his injuries, but he was there in the dugout, supporting his teammates and studying the Athletics' pitchers from the sidelines.

As the game progressed, the Dodgers were having a hard time cracking the Athletics' defense. The A's ace, Dennis Eckersley, was on top of his game, shutting down the Dodgers' offense. As the innings rolled by, the Dodgers' chances looked increasingly bleak.

Then came the bottom of the ninth. The Dodgers were down 4-3, and Eckersley, known for his ability to close out games, was on the mound. But then, something unexpected happened. Dodgers' manager Tommy Lasorda decided to take a gamble. He looked down the bench, locked eyes with Gibson, and gave him a nod. Despite the pain, Gibson rose to his feet and slowly limped towards the batter's box.

The crowd erupted as they saw number 23 step into the on-deck circle. Gibson, gritting his teeth against the pain, picked up his bat and made his way to the plate. Eckersley eyed him warily from the mound, and the showdown began.

The at-bat was a battle of wills. Gibson, clearly in pain, fought off pitch after pitch. Eckersley was relentless, not giving Gibson anything easy to hit. The count went full - three balls and two strikes. Eckersley wound up and delivered what he hoped would be the final pitch of the game.

Gibson swung with all the strength he could muster. The crack of the bat echoed through the stadium as the ball soared high into the right-field stands. Gibson had done it! He had hit a two-run homer to win the game for the Dodgers. He limped around the bases, pumping his fist in triumph, as the crowd went wild. The 'impossible' had happened, and Kirk Gibson became a legend.

The rest of the World Series seemed to ride on the wave of Gibson's extraordinary home run. The Dodgers went on to win the series in five games, but it was that moment - Gibson's impossible home run - that everyone remembers. It was a tale of perseverance, determination, and an unyielding belief in oneself.

Gibson's remarkable home run left an indelible mark on the history of the sport. But perhaps more importantly, it became a symbol of triumph over adversity. His determination to play, despite the pain, and his ability to deliver when it mattered most, was a testament to his character and spirit. His story is a lesson in perseverance, a reminder that even when the odds seem insurmountable, we should never stop trying.

Gibson's story isn't just about a single magical moment in the 1988 World Series. It's a story that began years before in Michigan, where a young athlete chose baseball over football and worked tirelessly to hone his skills. It's a story of a player who, despite injuries and setbacks, never lost faith in his abilities.

In the years that followed that iconic World Series, Gibson's fame grew, but he remained a humble and hard-working athlete. He went on to have a successful career as a coach and manager, always committed to sharing his love of the game and his never-give-up attitude with the next generation of players.

Gibson once said, "There's no one exactly like you. You have to believe in yourself." These words, just like his miraculous home run, continue to inspire young players worldwide, proving that self-belief and determination can help us overcome even the toughest challenges.

Gibson's legacy extends far beyond that one unforgettable night at Dodgers Stadium. His story continues to inspire athletes of all ages to believe in themselves and to understand the power of perseverance. The story of Kirk Gibson's impossible home run is more than a baseball story - it's a life lesson in courage, determination, and the strength of the human spirit.

Gibson's story serves as a reminder to all young sports enthusiasts that setbacks and obstacles are part of the journey. It's about picking yourself up, time and again, even when the circumstances seem challenging. It's about having faith in your abilities and never giving up. And most importantly, it's about understanding that real victory comes not just from winning but from the courage to keep going despite the odds.

So, as we move forward in our journey through the most amazing baseball stories of all time, let's remember Gibson's lesson: no matter the obstacles in our path, with determination and self-belief, we can hit our own home runs.

# Chapter Eight:

# Cal Ripken Jr.'s Ironman Streak

Calvin Edwin Ripken Jr., or as we know him, Cal Ripken Jr., was born into a baseball-loving family in Maryland in 1960. His father, Cal Sr., was a long-time coach and manager in the Major Leagues, mostly with the Baltimore Orioles. From a young age, Cal Jr. and his brother Billy, who also went on to become a professional player, were steeped in the world of baseball.

It wasn't just a game for the Ripkens. It was a way of life, a passion that was passed down from father to sons. As a youngster, Cal Jr. didn't just dream of becoming a professional baseball player; he lived it, practiced it, and breathed it, every single day. The field was his playground, and the bat and ball were his favorite toys.

Cal Ripken Jr.'s journey to the big leagues was a testament to hard work and dedication. He was drafted by the Baltimore Orioles, his hometown team, in the second round of the 1978 Major League Baseball Draft. After several years of honing his skills in the minor leagues, he made his Major League debut on August 10, 1981.

The following year, in 1982, Ripken was moved to shortstop, a position he would come to redefine over his career. Standing at 6'4", he was taller than most shortstops. However, his quick reflexes, arm strength, and adept reading of the game made him an exceptional player in this position.

While Ripken was an impressive player, racking up awards and accolades, including the Rookie of the Year in 1982 and the American League's Most Valuable Player in 1983 and 1991, what set him apart was not just his talent, but his extraordinary durability and love for the game. This brings us to the remarkable feat that he is most known for - his incredible "Ironman" streak.

The "Ironman" streak began on May 30, 1982. On that day, Ripken played in what would be the first of a record-breaking 2,632 consecutive games. This streak would continue for 16 years, becoming one of the most remarkable feats in professional sports.

At the time, the record for most consecutive games played was held by the legendary Lou Gehrig, who had played in 2,130 consecutive games, a record that had stood for 56 years and was considered unbreakable. But Ripken was about to change that.

Ripken didn't set out to break Gehrig's record. He simply believed in giving his best every day and playing every game as if it were his last. "I think the most important thing of all for any team is a winning attitude. The coaches must have it. The players must have it. The managers must have it. Everyone in the organization must have it. Our number one job is to win," he would say.

Injuries, fatigue, or tough schedules never deterred him. Every day, he would go out onto the field and give it his all, playing with the same enthusiasm and determination as he had since his childhood days.

By the late 1980s, Ripken's streak had started to attract attention. As he inched closer to Gehrig's record, the baseball world watched with anticipation and awe. Critics were skeptical and considered the record untouchable, but Cal carried on, consistent and unwavering.

Despite the mounting pressure and media attention, Ripken remained focused. He played each game with dedication, refusing to let anything distract him. He'd often say, "I go out there to play, and that's what I enjoy."

It was on September 6, 1995, in front of a home crowd at Camden Yards in Baltimore, that Ripken made history. In the fifth inning of the game against the California Angels, he fielded a routine grounder and threw it to first base for the out. It was a simple, uncomplicated play, but it was the one that officially broke Gehrig's record. The crowd roared as Ripken's consecutive games played tally climbed to 2,131. The "Iron Man" of baseball had done the impossible.

As soon as the game became official in the fifth inning, the celebration began. The game paused, and Ripken embarked on a victory lap around the stadium, high-fiving fans, and soaking in the love and admiration of the baseball world. The applause lasted for over 22 minutes, one of the longest standing ovations in professional sports history.

But Ripken didn't stop at 2,131. He continued his streak for another three years. On September 20, 1998, he voluntarily ended the streak at 2,632 games, choosing to sit out a game against the New York Yankees. The "Iron Man" streak had come to an end, but Cal Ripken Jr.'s place in baseball history was firmly cemented.

The streak might have ended, but Ripken's career was far from over. He continued to play with the same enthusiasm and dedication he had shown throughout his career. In 2001, after 21 seasons, all with the Baltimore Orioles, Ripken decided to retire. His farewell tour around the Major League ballparks was a heartfelt tribute to a player who had given so much to the game.

As Ripken walked away from his playing career, he left behind a legacy that extended beyond his impressive statistics and records. His love for the game, his relentless work ethic, and his remarkable endurance inspired millions. Ripken showed the world that you could achieve incredible things with perseverance and passion.

After retiring, Ripken didn't leave the world of baseball. He devoted himself to teaching the sport to younger generations, hoping to instill the same love and respect for the game that he had. He established the Cal Ripken, Sr. Foundation, in memory of his father, to help young people, particularly those from disadvantaged backgrounds, through baseball and softball-themed programs.

Cal Ripken Jr.'s story is an inspiring tale of passion, dedication, and perseverance. His "Iron Man" streak is a testament to what can be achieved with a never-give-up attitude. He played every single one of those 2,632 games with all his heart, showing the world that it's not just about ability, but also about attitude.

Ripken once said, "I'd like to think that the actions we take today will allow others in the future to discover the beauty of the game that we love." His actions on and off the field have undoubtedly fulfilled this wish, inspiring countless youngsters to discover and love the game of baseball.

As we continue our journey, let's take with us this lesson from Cal Ripken Jr.: With dedication and a never-give-up attitude, we can create our own unbreakable streaks in life.

# Chapter Nine:

# Hank Aaron's Record-Breaking Career: The Hammer

ank Aaron's journey to becoming one of the greatest baseball players in history begins in the most humble of circumstances. Born on February 5, 1934, in a poor neighborhood of Mobile, Alabama, Aaron, along with his seven siblings, was raised by parents Herbert and Estella Aaron. They were the descendants of African Americans who, for generations, had faced racial discrimination and economic hardship in the Deep South. However, the young Hank Aaron was never defined by his circumstances. Instead, he sought refuge and joy in a simple game that would change his life forever: baseball.

Young Hank was obsessed with baseball. Living in a house his father built with salvage materials, there was no money for luxuries such as baseball equipment. Despite this, Hank found a way. He would fashion bats and balls out of materials he could find, like broom handles and bottle caps, and would spend hours practicing his swing and perfecting his batting skills.

The environment around him was challenging. This was the era of segregation, and the racial prejudice was pervasive. However, Hank was not to be deterred. As he'd later recount, "I had my own little world, and that was to become a professional baseball player."

From his makeshift games in his backyard to his time playing for a semi-pro team, the Mobile Black Bears, and later his high school team, Aaron demonstrated an undeniable passion and talent for the sport. He developed a powerful swing, quick reflexes, and an extraordinary eye for the ball, talents that would take him places beyond his modest neighborhood.

In 1951, a significant opportunity came Aaron's way. He quit high school and began his professional career in the Negro Leagues with the Indianapolis Clowns. He was just 18 years old. His time in the Negro Leagues was short but impactful. Aaron's batting prowess became evident. In a few months, he was hitting a remarkable .366 and led the team to victory in the Negro League World Series.

His performance wasn't unnoticed. In June 1952, the Boston Braves, a Major League Baseball team, purchased Aaron's contract. The Braves recognized the diamond in the rough they had discovered, a player who was to change the course of baseball history.

After being signed by the Boston Braves, Aaron spent a couple of years in the minor leagues honing his skills. He batted .362 in his last year in the minors and was ready to make his mark on Major League Baseball. Unfortunately, a severe ankle injury sidelined him before he could play a game. But fate had something else in store for Aaron. Due to an injury to the Braves' starting left fielder, Aaron made his major league debut in 1954.

Right from his first year, Aaron showed exceptional talent. Despite his initial struggles, he soon started delivering consistent performances. He had an average of .280, hit 13 home runs and drove in 69 runs in his rookie season. His powerful swing, speed, and acumen on the field soon earned him the nickname "The Hammer."

In the following years, Aaron's performances just kept getting better. By 1957, he was one of the most feared batters in the league. That year, Aaron won his only Most Valuable Player award and led the Milwaukee Braves to their first World Series championship. The Braves defeated the New York Yankees in seven games, with Aaron hitting .393 with three home runs and seven RBI.

Hank Aaron's career was not without challenges. In particular, the racist threats and hate mail he received, especially during his pursuit of Babe Ruth's record, were appalling. But Aaron's resilience was unyielding. He responded with dignity, grace, and exceptional performances on the field. His courage during this period was as impressive as his athletic skills.

By the end of the 1960s, Aaron had established himself as one of the most consistent hitters in the history of baseball. He had notched up more than 500 home runs, had a career batting average of over .300, and was widely regarded as one of the greatest players of his generation. Yet, he was not done. Aaron was on the cusp of breaking one of the most hallowed records in all of sports - Babe Ruth's career home run record.

In the early 1970s, as Aaron was approaching his late thirties, an age when many players start to decline, he found himself on the brink of history. He was closing in on one of the most sacred records in American sports – Babe Ruth's career total of 714 home runs. As Aaron steadily chipped away at the record, the entire nation watched with bated breath.

The 1973 season ended with Aaron hitting 40 home runs, leaving him just one shy of Ruth's record. Throughout the winter, he received a torrent of letters, both encouraging and threatening. This was a difficult time for Aaron, who found himself under immense pressure, not just due to the historical magnitude of the record he was chasing, but also the intense racism he had to face in the process.

Despite the external pressures, Aaron kept his focus. The 1974 season began, and on April 4th, he tied Babe Ruth's record with a home run in his very first at-bat of the season. Four days later, on April 8, in front of a home crowd in Atlanta and millions watching on television, Aaron hit a fourth-inning pitch over the left field wall for home run number 715. As he rounded the bases, the crowd erupted in applause, the noise was deafening. Hammerin' Hank had done it; he had broken Babe Ruth's record.

Aaron finished his career with the Milwaukee Brewers, retiring in 1976. His records were astounding. Over his career, he had racked up 755 home runs, a record that stood until 2007. He still holds records for the most career RBI (2,297), total bases (6,856), and extra-base hits (1,477). More than just statistics, Aaron's career was a testament to consistent excellence, longevity, and a relentless drive to succeed.

After retiring from his playing career, Aaron didn't move away from baseball; rather, he continued to contribute to the sport in different ways. He joined the Atlanta Braves front office as an executive, working on promoting the sport among African American youth.

Aaron also established the Hank Aaron Chasing the Dream Foundation to help children with limited resources and great potential. He had once been a kid with a big dream himself, playing with a stick and a bottle cap in the streets of Mobile. Aaron knew the power of dreams, but also understood that not every child is given the same opportunities. His foundation awarded scholarships to children across the country to nurture their talents and help them chase their dreams, just like he did.

One of his biggest contributions to baseball post-retirement was the institution of the Hank Aaron Award in 1999. This award is given annually to the best overall offensive performers in the American and National League. It serves as a constant reminder of Aaron's exceptional career and the high standards he set in baseball.

Aaron continued to be a tireless advocate for racial equality. He spoke candidly about the racism he faced during his playing career and fought to promote diversity within the sport. His influence helped bring more African Americans into the game, both on the field and in the administrative offices.

To understand the full impact of Hank Aaron's career, one must look beyond the statistics and records. Yes, he was one of the greatest baseball players of all time, but his contributions to the sport and society are immeasurable. His story is one of breaking barriers, of endurance in the face of adversity, and of staying true to one's dreams, no matter how impossible they may seem.

In the end, Hank Aaron was not just a baseball player. He was a symbol of enduring courage, a testament to the power of perseverance, and an inspiration to countless people both within and outside the world of baseball. As we look back on his record-breaking career, we are reminded of his strength, his dignity, and the incredible impact he had on the game and the nation. He truly was, and always will be, 'The Hammer.'

Hank Aaron's legacy extends far beyond the baseball field. He has been a crucial figure in the fight for racial equality in sports and society. Despite the racial abuse he endured during his career, Aaron remained dignified and committed to equality. Post-retirement, Aaron was an ambassador for the sport, a respected executive, and a philanthropist. His career and life story continue to inspire countless people, reinforcing the values of resilience, determination, and integrity.

We hope this chapter has offered you a glimpse into the extraordinary life and career of Hank Aaron, a man who, against all odds, carved his name in baseball history. His story is one of not just talent, but tenacity and courage, proving that no obstacle is too great if one has the determination to overcome it.

# Chapter Ten:

# A League of Their Own: The All-American Girls Professional Baseball League

Imagine, if you will, the year 1943. The world is in the throes of World War II, and many of America's able-bodied men, including numerous baseball players, are fighting overseas. A fear begins to grow among baseball enthusiasts and executives. With many of the sport's best talents away at war, could this beloved national pastime continue to flourish? Enter Philip K. Wrigley, chewing gum mogul and owner of the Chicago Cubs. Wrigley had an idea that was nothing short of revolutionary - an all-women's professional baseball league.

Now, for some context, it's important to remember that women playing baseball was not widely accepted at the time. Women were often relegated to the sidelines, allowed only to cheer for the men playing the game. The concept of women playing professional baseball, competing in their own league, was almost unheard of. However, as the saying goes, "necessity is the mother of invention." With Major League Baseball's future uncertain due to the war, Wrigley's idea didn't seem so far-fetched anymore. In fact, it became a necessity.

The All-American Girls Professional Baseball League (AAGPBL) was established in 1943. Initially, Wrigley invited softball players from around the country to try out. The first tryouts were held in Chicago's Wrigley Field, with over 200 women attending. Of these, only 60 were chosen, forming four teams - the Rockford Peaches, the Racine Belles, the South Bend Blue Sox, and the Kenosha Comets. These women were about to make history and change the face of baseball forever.

Let's take a moment to dive into what it was like to be a player in this groundbreaking league. The women of the AAGPBL were not only athletes; they were expected to embody the societal norms of femininity as well. This meant attending charm school, adhering to a strict beauty regimen, and even playing in skirts! The dichotomy of this situation is quite intriguing - these women were pushing boundaries, shattering stereotypes, and at the same time, expected to maintain their traditional roles in society.

Despite the challenges, the women of the AAGPBL played with extraordinary skill and determination. The games were thrilling, filled with the same joy, excitement, and competitive spirit found in any men's league. The inaugural season saw the Racine Belles clinch the championship, but the real victory was the establishment and success of the league itself.

The AAGPBL continued to operate for the next eleven years, even after World War II had ended and men's baseball had resumed. During this period, the league expanded, peaking at ten teams in 1948, and over 600 women got the opportunity to play professional baseball. Although the league eventually dissolved in 1954, it left a significant mark on the history of baseball. The women of the AAGPBL had shown that they were more than capable of playing professional baseball, and they did so with grace, athleticism, and determination.

To truly understand the impact of the AAGPBL, we must look at the broader picture. These women pushed societal boundaries and paved the way for future generations. They stood in the face of adversity and proved that women could excel in a sport dominated by men. They showed little girls everywhere that they, too, could play baseball, and that their dreams were valid and achievable. In many ways, the women of the AAGPBL were more than just baseball players - they were pioneers, champions of women's rights, and an inspiration to all.

The legacy of the All-American Girls Professional Baseball League is an essential part of baseball history, and so it's only fitting that we spend some time delving into the lives and achievements of a few of the incredible women who made up the league.

Doris "Sammye" Sams, for example, was a multi-talented player who excelled both as a pitcher and an outfielder. Hailing from Knoxville, Tennessee, Sammye began her career with the Muskegon Lassies in 1946. Her illustrious career spanned eight seasons, during which she received multiple accolades, including being named Player of the Year twice. She was an all-rounder, pitching a no-hitter in one game, and hitting multiple home runs in another. Sammye embodied the spirit of the league—resilient, skillful, and passionate about the sport.

There was also Connie Wisniewski, aptly nicknamed the "Iron Woman" of the AAGPBL. Connie began her career as an outfielder, but her extraordinary pitching skills soon took center stage. During the 1945 season, Connie pitched an astounding 2,028 innings and had a winning streak of 13 games, making her one of the most formidable pitchers of her time. She played with grit and determination, truly living up to her nickname.

However, the league was not just made up of American players. There were also women from Canada who played a significant role in the AAGPBL. One such player was Mary "Bonnie" Baker, a Canadian catcher who played for the South Bend Blue Sox and the Kalamazoo Lassies. Bonnie was an exceptional player, even earning a spot in the All-Star team in the league's first year. Later, she became the first woman manager of the league, further cementing her place in baseball history.

The stories of these women, and so many more like them, paint a vivid picture of what the AAGPBL represented—an opportunity for women to break barriers, display their talent, and share their love for baseball. The courage and determination of these women not only changed the sport but also had a profound impact on society.

Despite the league's eventual disbandment in 1954, the legacy of the AAGPBL lives on. It took decades, but in 1988, the Baseball Hall of Fame in Cooperstown, New York, finally recognized the league and its players. A permanent display was installed to honor the women of the AAGPBL and their contribution to baseball. The recognition was long overdue but marked a significant step in acknowledging women's role in the sport.

In 1992, the AAGPBL stepped back into the spotlight with the release of "A League of Their Own," a film directed by Penny Marshall and starring Tom Hanks, Geena Davis, and Madonna. The movie, though fictionalized, is based on the real stories of the women who played in the AAGPBL. It reminded people of a forgotten piece of baseball history and brought the stories of these pioneering women to a new generation.

The All-American Girls Professional Baseball League was more than just a sporting event; it was a historical movement that changed the perception of women in sports. It is a testament to the courage and resilience of women who dared to step onto the baseball field, challenge societal norms, and inspire future generations of female athletes. Their legacy continues to shape the world of sports today, reminding us all of the power of perseverance and the love of the game.

So, as we celebrate the most amazing baseball stories of all time, we tip our caps to the brave women of the All-American Girls

Professional Baseball League. Their remarkable journey is not just a baseball story; it is a tale of trailblazers, of barrier breakers, and of change makers. They are the epitome of what can be achieved when passion, skill, and the audacity to challenge the status quo combine. Their story teaches us that no field—be it a baseball field or otherwise—is beyond reach due to one's gender.

To truly appreciate the All-American Girls Professional Baseball League, it is important to understand the era in which it was born. In the 1940s, women's rights were a far cry from what we see today. The traditional roles of women were still firmly in place, and societal norms dictated that a woman's place was in the home. Against this backdrop, the AAGPBL was a beacon of change, a tangible sign that women were just as capable as men, both on and off the baseball field.

In a time when women had limited professional sports opportunities, the AAGPBL showed the world that women could hold their own in a male-dominated industry. These women were not just players; they were ambassadors of change. They proved to the world that women could excel at sports just as well as men, laying the foundation for future generations of women in sports.

The AAGPBL was also a unifying force. During the difficult war years, the league brought joy and entertainment to thousands of fans across America. Families flocked to the stadiums, eager to see their favorite teams play. The games brought a much-needed reprieve from the hardships of war and provided a sense of unity and national pride. The players became role models for countless young girls who aspired to play baseball and served as symbols of hope during those turbulent times.

While the AAGPBL disbanded in 1954, its influence did not fade away. The players continued to inspire and pave the way for future female athletes. Today, we see women participating in a wide range of sports, competing professionally, and breaking records. While there is still a long way to go in achieving gender equality in sports, we have the players of the AAGPBL to thank for taking those first courageous steps.

The AAGPBL stands as a testimony to what can be achieved with resilience and determination. The players' courage in overcoming societal norms, their hard work, and their sheer love for the game are truly inspiring. They not only changed the face of baseball but also influenced societal perceptions of women in sports.

In the words of Penny Marshall, director of the movie, "A League of Their Own," - "These women made a significant contribution to the history of baseball and to the women's movement, and they've been overlooked. They tell us that if you tell a girl she can't play ball, she might believe it. But if you tell her she can, she just might change the world."

The tale of the All-American Girls Professional Baseball League is indeed a tale of their own, a tale of immense courage, skill, and determination. As we recount the extraordinary stories of baseball, we pay tribute to these women, who, with their spirit and love for the game, changed baseball and the world forever. As we close this chapter, let's carry forward the lessons we've learned from these extraordinary women - to always strive for our dreams, to break barriers, and above all, to always love the game we play.

# Chapter Eleven:
# The Unforgettable Catch by Jim Edmonds

Once upon a time, in the bustling city of St. Louis, there lived a baseball legend named Jim Edmonds. To the baseball fans of the city, he was not just a player; he was a magician, a ballet dancer, a superhero—all rolled into one! He would leap and dash, pirouette and dive, all to catch a tiny sphere flying through the sky. But of all his spectacular displays, one stood head and shoulders above the rest. This chapter is dedicated to that unforgettable catch, a catch that is still etched in the memories of baseball fans across the world.

Jim was born on June 27, 1970, in Fullerton, California. His love for baseball started at an early age, as if the sport was ingrained in his DNA. His father, who was a coach for a local little league team, played a significant role in nurturing his passion for the sport. They spent countless hours in their backyard, with Jim swinging at pitches thrown by his dad, both lost in their shared love for the game.

Growing up, he idolized players like Reggie Jackson and Mickey Mantle, dreaming of one day stepping onto the field and making his mark just like his heroes. His family would often tell the story of how little Jim, barely big enough to swing a bat, would stand in front of the TV and imitate the swings of the greats.

Jim's childhood was not without struggles. His family wasn't wealthy, and they often had to make do with limited resources. But these difficulties only served to strengthen Jim's resolve. He took the lessons he learned from baseball - resilience, perseverance, and hard work - and applied them to his life.

His family couldn't afford the best baseball gear, but that didn't stop him. He would practice with worn-out gloves and patched-up balls, making the best out of what he had. It wasn't about the equipment; it was about the passion, the dedication, and the love for the game that made him stand out.

As Jim grew older, his skill on the baseball field became more evident. He played in high school and was eventually offered a scholarship to play at the University of California, Irvine. He didn't let the opportunity pass him by. He saw it as a stepping stone towards his dream of playing in the major leagues.

Now, let's fast forward to Jim's Major League career. Our story takes place on June 10, 1997, in the cavernous Anaheim Stadium, the home to the Anaheim Angels. The Kansas City

Royals were the visiting team, and the game was as intense as a final game of the World Series. The Angels, for whom Jim Edmonds was playing, were trying to maintain their lead in the game. The fans, holding their breath with anticipation, watched with bated breath as each pitch was thrown, each bat swung, each base rounded.

In the top of the fifth inning, the Royals were at bat. David Howard, the Royals' shortstop, was on the plate, ready to swing. On the mound for the Angels was pitcher Dennis Springer, a crafty knuckleballer known for his tricky pitches. As Springer wound up and released the ball, Howard, anticipating the pitch, swung his bat with all his might. There was a loud crack as the bat connected with the ball, and in an instant, it was hurtling towards deep center field.

The moment the ball left the bat, Jim Edmonds, stationed at center field, sprang into action. This was his moment, his stage. He was known for his spectacular catches, but this one, this one was going to be extraordinary.

With the ball soaring over his head, Edmonds took off. His eyes locked onto the rapidly disappearing ball, his feet pounding the grass as he sprinted towards the warning track. There was no room for error, no time to hesitate. Edmonds was racing not just against the ball, but against time itself.

As the ball continued its high, arching path, it seemed to hang in the air, as if challenging Edmonds to reach it. The crowd held its collective breath, their eyes glued to the figure running with all his might on the field.

And then, in a display of sheer athleticism and absolute commitment, Edmonds launched himself into the air, his body fully extended, his back to the home plate, his eyes still glued to the ball. It was a leap of faith, a testament to Edmonds' belief in his ability, and a split second later, his gloved hand closed around the ball.

The stadium erupted into cheers as Edmonds tumbled on the grass, holding up his glove to show the ball nestled securely inside. He had done it! He had made the catch! It was a moment of pure, unadulterated joy for the Angels' fans and a moment of awe for every baseball lover watching.

The catch was replayed countless times, not just on that day, but in the years that followed. It became a symbol of determination and athleticism, a reminder that with grit, skill, and a whole lot of courage, the seemingly impossible could be achieved.

Jim Edmonds' catch was not just an unforgettable moment in a baseball game; it was a life lesson, a story to inspire every kid who dreams of making that spectacular catch, scoring that winning run, or throwing that perfect pitch. It was a testament to the fact that in baseball, as in life, magic can happen in the blink of an eye.

His catch was not just a feat of athleticism, but it was also a work of art, a ballet performed on a baseball field. And like every great piece of art, it touched the hearts of those who witnessed it. The fans, the players, the coaches - everyone present that day had a story to tell, a memory to cherish.

Back in the locker room, Edmonds' teammates gathered around him, patting him on the back, their faces lit up with excitement and admiration. It wasn't just about the catch anymore, it was about the spirit it embodied - the spirit of not giving up, of giving everything you've got, and of rising to the occasion.

But in the midst of all the excitement and celebration, Edmonds remained modest. When asked about his catch, he simply shrugged and said, "I was just doing my job."

That was the essence of Jim Edmonds. He never considered himself a superstar or a hero. He was just a player who loved the game and gave it his all. But in doing so, he inspired countless others, especially the young fans who watched him play.

Kids across the country began emulating Edmonds. In backyards, in school playgrounds, in little league games, they would try to recreate the magic of Edmonds' catch. They would run and leap, tumble and dive, all in an attempt to catch the ball just like their hero had done.

Teachers and parents would use Edmonds' catch as an example when talking about dedication, hard work, and perseverance. They would tell their kids, "Look at Jim Edmonds. He never gave up, and look what he achieved. You can do the same if you put your mind to it."

Years have passed since that unforgettable day in Anaheim Stadium, but the memory of the catch lives on. It lives on in the heart of every baseball fan, in the dreams of every kid holding a baseball glove, and in the spirit of the game itself.

So here's to Jim Edmonds and his unforgettable catch. Here's to the magic of baseball, and the inspiration it provides to all of us. As we continue to watch and play the game we love, let us strive to embody the spirit of that catch, and in doing so, let us create our own unforgettable moments.

And so, our tale of Jim Edmonds' spectacular catch comes to a close. But remember, every time you step onto a field, every time you grip a bat or a ball, you carry with you the potential to create your own unforgettable moment, just like Jim Edmonds did. So play with all your heart, give it all you've got, and who knows? Maybe one day, you will be the one inspiring the world with your own incredible catch.

And remember, in the words of Jim Edmonds himself, "I was just doing my job." It was this humble mindset, this unwavering dedication to the game, that made him a legend. So, whether you're on the field or off, always strive to do your job to the best of your ability. And who knows, you might just make an unforgettable catch of your own.

Until then, keep dreaming, keep playing, and keep believing. Because in the game of baseball, just like in life, amazing things can happen if you just keep your eye on the ball.

The end of the chapter is here, but the story continues. There are more inspiring tales of determination, of talent, and of unforgettable moments. So stick around, keep reading, and let the magic of baseball sweep you off your feet. And remember, every game, every play, every catch, is a story waiting to be told.

# Chapter Twelve:

# Boston Red Sox Break the Curse

L ike a story lifted straight from a fairy tale, a saga filled with sorrows, setbacks, trials, and finally, the ultimate triumph, the tale of the Boston Red Sox in 2004 is one for the ages. It's a testament to the power of perseverance, belief, and an unwavering will to win. To truly understand the depths of joy felt on that fateful day in October 2004, we need to start our journey from the beginning of the year and unravel the rich tapestry of emotions, the ebbs, and flows of the regular season.

The 2004 season for the Boston Red Sox began like any other, but with a quiet whisper of optimism that this could be the year. The year when the ominous "Curse of the Bambino," a ghost that had loomed over the team for 86 long years, could finally be lifted. The curse began in 1919 when the Red Sox's star player, Babe Ruth, famously nicknamed "The Bambino," was sold to their bitter rivals, the New York Yankees. The Red Sox, who had been one of the most successful teams in the league, suddenly found themselves in a championship drought that lasted decades. The pain was especially acute because their rivals, the Yankees, racked up championship after championship. But in 2004, there was a glimmer of hope that things might be about to change.

The 2004 Red Sox team was a formidable group, a blend of seasoned veterans and young blood, all talented and driven. Managed by Terry Francona, players like David Ortiz, Manny Ramirez, Curt Schilling, and Pedro Martinez became household names, their performances throughout the season keeping the fans' hopes alive. The team started the season strong, showing their competitors they meant business. Their 98-64 record by the end of the regular season reflected the Red Sox's strength, securing their spot in the postseason.

As fate would have it, the Red Sox found themselves up against their rivals, the New York Yankees, in the American League Championship Series (ALCS). The rivalry between these two teams is one of the most storied in baseball history, adding an extra layer of anticipation and intensity to the face-off. However, the series began disastrously for the Red Sox, losing the first three games. It seemed like the ghost of the Bambino was about to claim another year of Red Sox dreams.

But then, something extraordinary happened. Faced with the possibility of elimination, the Red Sox came alive in Game 4. With a heart-stopping steal of second base by Dave Roberts and a clutch hit from Bill Mueller, they managed to tie the game, later winning it in extra innings. The tide began to turn. The team that was written off just a day earlier was suddenly back in the fight.

Over the next three games, the Red Sox played some of the best baseball in their history. Ortiz, the powerhouse hitter, took the Yankees to task, earning him the nickname "Senor Octubre" or "Mr. October." Curt Schilling pitched a remarkable Game 6, despite an injured ankle that left his sock soaked in blood, an event that has been immortalized as the "Bloody Sock" game. The team's spirit was indomitable; their belief in themselves and each other was unwavering. The impossible happened. The Red Sox won four games in a row, becoming the first team in MLB history to win a seven-game series after being down 0-3. The victory was sweet, but there was still one hurdle left to conquer—the World Series.

With the St. Louis Cardinals standing in their path to glory, the Red Sox knew they had their work cut out for them. But undaunted by the challenge, the Red Sox strode onto the field, bolstered by their unprecedented comeback victory against the Yankees. The World Series was within their grasp, and they were determined not to let this opportunity slip.

From the first pitch of the World Series, the Red Sox were a team transformed. Their earlier games had showcased their skill, but these games revealed their heart. Ortiz's booming bat continued to perform, racking up hits and sending balls soaring into the stands. Manny Ramirez played the series of his life, his game-winning RBI in Game 1 setting the tone for what was to come.

The Cardinals, while a formidable opponent, couldn't stifle the momentum that the Red Sox had gathered. Each pitch, each swing, each catch was executed with precision. By Game 2, the Red Sox were in full swing. Curt Schilling, ankle heavily bandaged following his heroic ALCS performance, took the mound. Despite his injury, he pitched a near-flawless game, helping the Red Sox secure another victory.

As the series moved to Busch Stadium in St. Louis for Game 3, the Red Sox showed no signs of slowing down. Pedro Martinez, another Red Sox ace, took the helm. He weaved through the Cardinals lineup, his pitches a dizzying array of speed and precision. The defense, too, was on point, snuffing out any offensive glimmers the Cardinals hoped to ignite. The Red Sox won Game 3, pushing the Cardinals to the brink of elimination.

October 27th, 2004, Game 4 of the World Series, is a day that will forever be etched in the annals of baseball history. The Red Sox had the chance to secure their first championship in 86 years. The air was electric with anticipation.

Red Sox's Derek Lowe took the mound, the weight of countless dreams resting on his shoulders. However, he didn't let the pressure get to him. Instead, he pitched one of the best games of his career, holding the Cardinals scoreless for seven innings. Meanwhile, the Red Sox offense chipped away at the Cardinals' resolve, scoring runs off hits by Trot Nixon and Johnny Damon.

In the end, closer Keith Foulke took the mound in the ninth inning, securing the final outs and clinching an unforgettable 3-0 victory. The players poured onto the field, the stadium erupted, and fans across the world cheered. The Boston Red Sox, after an 86-year drought, were finally World Series Champions.

The 2004 season was a turning point, not just for the Boston Red Sox but for all of baseball. It reminded us of why we love sports. It's not just about the scores, the statistics, or the trophies. It's about the human spirit, about believing even when the odds are stacked against us, and about coming together to achieve the impossible. The 2004 Boston Red Sox embodied all this and more, providing a thrilling season that will continue to inspire for generations to come.

From the roller coaster of the regular season to the nail-biting playoffs and the triumphant World Series, the journey of the 2004 Red Sox is a testament to determination, teamwork, and the power of self-belief. They showed that no matter how formidable the challenge, with perseverance and courage, any curse can be broken.

With the curse finally lifted, the city of Boston breathed a collective sigh of relief, their joy mirrored by Red Sox fans worldwide. The team that had come to be known as the "lovable losers" were losers no more. They were champions, their victory a beacon of hope for anyone who has ever dared to dream of overcoming the insurmountable. Their story is a lasting testament to the spirit of baseball, and to the incredible journey that sports can take us on.

In the aftermath of their win, the streets of Boston were filled with jubilant fans, their joyous cries filling the autumn air. Cheers of "Red Sox Nation!" could be heard far into the night, the celebrations continuing for days. The team was greeted as heroes upon their return to Boston, the victory parade drawing millions of fans who wanted to be part of this historic moment.

In the weeks and months that followed, stories emerged about the team and the players that had become legends. Ortiz, the powerhouse hitter who had been crucial to the Red Sox's success, was named the Most Valuable Player of the World Series, his impressive batting cementing his place in baseball history. Pedro Martinez, Curt Schilling, and Derek Lowe, the three pitchers who had stood tall against the Yankees and Cardinals, became synonymous with resilience and determination. And Manny Ramirez, with his game-winning RBI in the World Series opener, was celebrated for his undeniable talent and critical contribution to the team's victory.

Looking back, the 2004 season was filled with memorable moments. From the regular season's ups and downs, the unbelievable comeback in the ALCS, and the final, sweet victory of the World Series, it was a journey filled with drama, excitement, and heart. The curse had been a dark cloud over the Red Sox for nearly a century, but in its breaking, the team found light, proving to the world and to themselves that they were capable of great things.

Their victory was not just about a championship; it was about breaking barriers and changing the narrative. It was about every player who stepped onto the field, every fan who cheered them on, and every dream that was fulfilled when the final out was made.

In the history of baseball, there have been many incredible seasons, many fantastic teams, and many unforgettable games. But the story of the 2004 Boston Red Sox stands out. Their journey serves as a reminder that in the face of adversity, it's possible to rise, to fight, and to overcome.

The tale of the Boston Red Sox in 2004 is a story that transcends sports. It is a story of hope, resilience, and redemption. It is a testament to the power of dreams and the indomitable human spirit. The team's courage, determination, and belief in themselves and each other turned the tide of history, broke an 86-year old curse, and created a legacy that will inspire generations to come.

In their victory, the 2004 Boston Red Sox showed the world that anything is possible, that even the most persistent of curses can be broken. It was a magical season, a triumphant journey that continues to inspire and captivate, a story that reminds us all that in baseball, and in life, nothing is truly impossible.

# Chapter Thirteen:

# Mr. November: Derek Jeter's Legendary World Series

Derek Jeter, a name that echoes with glory and honor in the hallways of Yankee Stadium, is not just another baseball player. He's a legend, a beacon of steadfast leadership and immense talent, and this is the story of how he became Mr. November in one unforgettable World Series.

Born in 1974 in Pequannock, New Jersey, Derek was the elder of two children. His father, Dr. Sanderson Charles Jeter, a substance abuse counselor, and mother, Dorothy, an accountant, were strict disciplinarians. They made sure that young Derek and his sister, Sharlee, stayed focused on their academics, with a contract set at the beginning of each school year outlining acceptable grades and behavior.

Despite the rigid focus on studies, there was one passion that shone brightly in Derek's heart from a very young age - baseball. He fell in love with the sport, thanks to the influence of his grandmother, who was a passionate fan of the New York Yankees. When Derek was just four years old, he went to a Yankees game, and that was all it took for him to decide his dream. He wanted to be a shortstop for the New York Yankees.

And so began the journey of a boy with a big dream. Derek spent countless hours practicing, taking his baseball mitt everywhere he went. He played Little League and high school baseball, consistently standing out as a promising player. His parents were supportive, driving him to games and practices, always reminding him to balance his love for the sport with his schoolwork.

After an impressive high school career, Derek had the opportunity to attend the University of Michigan on a baseball scholarship, but the pull of his childhood dream was too strong. When the Yankees picked him as the sixth overall draft pick in 1992, he chose to forgo college and plunged headfirst into his dream.

In the initial years, the journey wasn't smooth. Derek struggled in his first professional season, but this was a young man fueled by a burning desire, someone who looked at setbacks as setups for comebacks. Slowly but surely, Derek began to make his mark, making his major league debut in 1995, and by the following year, he was the Yankees' starting shortstop.

The late 90s and early 2000s were a glorious era for the New York Yankees, and Derek Jeter was at the heart of it. The team's "Core Four", including Jeter, Mariano Rivera, Andy Pettitte, and Jorge Posada, were key to their success, helping the team win several World Series Championships.

However, it was the World Series in 2001 that etched Derek Jeter's name in baseball history forever and earned him the title of "Mr. November". To understand the magnitude of what Derek achieved, it's crucial to remember the context. The World Series of 2001 was being played under the shadow of the tragic 9/11 terrorist attacks. The city of New York and indeed, the entire nation, was grieving, and baseball, America's pastime, was a source of comfort and unity during those difficult times.

The Yankees were playing the Arizona Diamondbacks. It was Game 4, and the Yankees were trailing 2-1 in the series. In the bottom of the ninth inning, with the Yankees down by two runs, Tino Martinez hit a two-run homer, tying the game and pushing it into extra innings. This is where Derek Jeter's moment of magic occurred.

With the clock having ticked past midnight and the calendar flipping to November, Jeter stepped up to the plate in the bottom of the 10th inning. The crowd held its collective breath, the stadium, with its cheering fans and bright lights, sat on the edge of its seat. Jeter was a known clutch hitter, someone who you'd want at the plate when the game was on the line, and this was his moment.

Diamondbacks pitcher Byung-Hyun Kim was on the mound. Kim, a young and talented closer from South Korea, had a distinctive submarine delivery that was tough to hit. The first few pitches were a duel, with Jeter fouling off several attempts. The air was tense; the anticipation was like electricity coursing through the stadium.

Finally, Kim launched a slider towards the plate. Jeter saw his opportunity and swung with all his might. The crack of the bat echoed around the stadium, the sound every baseball player loves to hear, the sound of a perfect hit. The ball soared, arcing high into the right-field stands, and the Yankee Stadium erupted. Jeter had done it! He had won the game with a walk-off home run, a feat of strength, skill, and mental fortitude that etched him forever in World Series history.

Jeter circled the bases, his face a picture of elation and disbelief. As he rounded third and headed for home, his teammates poured out of the dugout, ready to mob him in celebration. The cheers from the crowd were deafening, drowning out even the loud thumps of his teammates' palms against his back. He had come through when it mattered the most, at the most challenging time for his city and his country. That moment transcended the sport of baseball and spoke to the human spirit's resilience, making Jeter not just a sports hero but a symbol of hope and resilience.

This wasn't just a home run, it was the first World Series home run hit in November, and it came off the bat of a kid from New Jersey who had always dreamed of being a Yankee. The nickname "Mr. November" was born, and Derek Jeter was immortalized as a clutch player, someone who delivered under the most intense pressure, someone who lived for moments like these.

Derek Jeter's legendary World Series moment was more than just an incredible sports achievement. It was a testament to his childhood dream, the countless hours of practice, the steadfast commitment to his team, and his unyielding determination to win. His parents, who once made him sign contracts about his school grades and behavior, were in the stands that night, brimming with pride at their son's accomplishment. His dream had not only become a reality, but he had also become a beacon of hope, a source of joy, and a symbol of resilience.

The 2001 World Series, even though it ultimately ended in a heartbreaking Game 7 loss for the Yankees, was forever marked by Derek Jeter's extraordinary moment. It was a testament to a man who, from a young age, set his sights on a dream and worked tirelessly to achieve it. It was a testament to the boy who held a baseball mitt in his hand and wished to play for the Yankees, who grew up to not only fulfill his dream but also became one of the greatest players in the team's storied history.

Years later, Jeter would say, "I love it when people doubt me. It makes me work harder to prove them wrong." And prove them wrong he did, time and time again, showing everyone that with hard work, dedication, and a never-give-up attitude, you could achieve anything, even hitting a walk-off home run in the World Series. The tale of Derek Jeter, Mr. November, is a testament to the power of dreams and the triumph of determination. His story is one that will inspire baseball fans and young dreamers for generations to come.

Even though that home run and his spectacular performance throughout the series didn't lead to a championship in 2001, Jeter's clutch moment in the World Series became emblematic of his entire career. Every time he stepped up to the plate, fans expected greatness, and he delivered more often than not.

In the subsequent seasons, Jeter continued to be a pillar of strength for the Yankees. Despite the ups and downs, the victories, and losses, his consistency and determination remained unshaken. He was named team captain in 2003, a position that hadn't been filled since Don Mattingly retired in 1995. It was a testament to Jeter's leadership both on and off the field.

His phenomenal career continued with the same dedication he showed in his early years, and he consistently performed at the highest level. He collected accolades and broke records, further establishing his legacy as one of baseball's greatest. In his 20-year Major League career, Jeter achieved a lifetime batting average of .310, accumulated 3,465 hits—sixth most in MLB history—and was a 14-time All-Star. His defensive prowess at shortstop, combined with his batting skills, made him one of the most well-rounded players in the game.

However, Jeter's success was never solely about his numbers. It was about his intangible qualities—the leadership, the work ethic, the love for the game, and the respect for his teammates and opponents alike. He played with heart, with a contagious joy that made others around him better.

It was these qualities that have perhaps left the most significant impact. Young players who watched Jeter play—watched his dedication, his grace under pressure, his sportsmanship—have been inspired to emulate him. He taught them not just about being great players, but about being great individuals, about playing with heart and respecting the game. In that sense, Jeter's influence reaches far beyond his own accomplishments. He has shaped the game and continues to inspire the next generation of players.

From his humble beginnings in Kalamazoo, Michigan, to his remarkable career with the New York Yankees, Derek Jeter, or Mr. November, as he will always be known, remains a symbol of what can be achieved with a dream, hard work, and unyielding determination. His story isn't just a baseball story; it's a story of dreaming big, of aiming for the stars, and not being afraid of the hard work it takes to get there.

By the end of his career, Jeter had not only become a Yankees legend but also a baseball icon. His number 2 jersey was retired by the Yankees, and he was inducted into the Baseball Hall of Fame in his first year of eligibility, receiving 99.7% of the votes– a fitting tribute to a man who had given so much to the sport.

Every time a kid steps onto a baseball field, dreaming of making it big, the story of Derek Jeter, of his journey from being a young boy in Kalamazoo with a dream to becoming Mr. November, serves as a guiding light. It is a story of perseverance, resilience, and unwavering faith in oneself. It is a story that will continue to inspire and captivate, reminding us all of the power of dreams and the magic of baseball.

# Chapter Fourteen:

# Bryce Harper: The Boy Wonder

In a small corner of Las Vegas, Nevada, a young boy of just three years was taking his first swing at a tee-ball. His parents watched as the bat connected with the ball and sent it sailing through the backyard. It was a moment that would mark the beginning of an extraordinary journey for Bryce Harper.

Bryce Aron Max Harper was born on October 16, 1992, to Ron and Sheri Harper. His parents were avid baseball fans, and their enthusiasm quickly rubbed off on young Bryce. They introduced him to the sport at a tender age, and by the time he was five, he was playing in a T-ball league with kids who were older than him. By the age of seven, Bryce was already playing travel baseball. In many ways, Bryce was not an ordinary kid; he had a burning passion for baseball that was rare for someone his age.

This passion drove Bryce to work harder than most kids. While others were playing video games or hanging out with friends, Bryce was in the backyard or at the local baseball field, practicing his swing or working on his pitching. His parents recognized his talent and were supportive, never missing a game or a practice. They became his first and biggest fans, cheering him on from the sidelines as he started to dominate the local leagues.

In his early teens, Bryce began turning heads in a big way. His extraordinary skills were far beyond those of his peers. His batting power was prodigious, he had a rocket arm, and his speed made him a terror on the base paths. But it was not just his raw talent that was impressive; it was also his understanding of the game. Bryce had a baseball IQ well beyond his years. He was not just playing; he was studying the game, absorbing it, living it.

In 2009, at the age of 16, Bryce made national headlines when he appeared on the cover of Sports Illustrated. The headline read, "Baseball's Chosen One," and the article compared him to LeBron James of baseball. Imagine that: a high school sophomore being compared to some of the greatest athletes in history. But that's how good Bryce was. That's how much potential he had. He was already being viewed as the future of baseball, and he hadn't even graduated from high school yet.

Around the same time, Bryce made another bold move that further demonstrated his commitment to his dream. He left high school after his sophomore year, got his General Equivalency Diploma (GED), and enrolled at the College of Southern Nevada. This move allowed him to be eligible for the Major League Baseball Draft a year earlier.

At the College of Southern Nevada, Bryce dominated the competition. He won the 2010 Golden Spikes Award, given annually to the best amateur baseball player in the United States. The scouts were all in agreement: Bryce Harper was the real deal. It was now just a matter of waiting until the MLB Draft to see where his journey would take him next.

Playing at the College of Southern Nevada proved to be a smart decision for Bryce. In the Scenic West Athletic Conference, he set records that stunned even his own coaches. He smashed 31 home runs, a new record that eclipsed the old one by 12. He had an impressive batting average of .443 and 98 RBIs. All of this, he accomplished in just 66 games.

His incredible performances caught the eyes of professional scouts from all over the country. Everyone wanted to see if this teenage phenomenon was the real deal. Many saw him as the most sought-after prospect since Alex Rodriguez, and that was saying a lot. At his games, the stands were filled with scouts, each holding a radar gun and a dream of seeing Bryce wear their team's jersey.

When the 2010 Major League Baseball Draft rolled around, Bryce didn't have to wait long to hear his name. He was picked first overall by the Washington Nationals. It was a dream come true. Bryce was on his way to the major leagues, and he was just 17.

But before he could step onto a major league field, there was work to be done. Bryce spent the next couple of years in the minor leagues, honing his skills and preparing for the big stage. The Nationals didn't want to rush him. They knew he was a once-in-a-generation talent and they wanted to do everything they could to help him reach his potential.

In 2012, the wait was finally over. Bryce was called up to the majors and he didn't disappoint. In his very first game, he got a double and showcased his impressive arm strength with a bullet of a throw from left field to home plate. Bryce was here, and he was ready to take the major leagues by storm.

His rookie season was nothing short of impressive. He was named an All-Star and won the National League Rookie of the Year award. Bryce was living up to the hype. His aggressive style of play, combined with his raw talent, made him a fan favorite. And he was just getting started.

Over the next few years, Bryce established himself as one of the best players in the league. He won the National League Most Valuable Player (MVP) award in 2015, becoming the youngest unanimous MVP in the history of Major League Baseball. His fiery passion for the game, his powerful swing, and his all-out effort on the field have made him a must-watch player. His jersey is one of the top sellers in the league and his face can be seen on billboards and in commercials all over the country.

Through all of this, Bryce has remained true to himself. He still plays the game with the same passion and intensity he had as a young boy in Las Vegas. He still studies the game, always looking for ways to improve. He still pushes himself, always striving to be the best.

Bryce Harper's journey from child prodigy to major league superstar is a testament to his talent, hard work, and perseverance. But more than that, it's a testament to his love for the game. From the backyard in Las Vegas to the major league fields, baseball has always been a part of Bryce's life. And if his career so far is any indication, he's set to leave a lasting legacy in the sport.

Bryce Harper's story is far from over. His career is still being written, with new chapters being added with each passing season. He continues to be one of the brightest stars in Major League Baseball and his impact goes beyond just his on-field performances. His love for the game, his determination to always improve, and his willingness to push the limits are qualities that inspire young players all over the world.

In 2019, another major milestone came in Bryce's career. After several successful seasons with the Nationals, Bryce became a free agent. This is a period when a player's contract with a team has ended, and they are free to negotiate and sign a new contract with any team. This was a significant moment, not just for Bryce, but for the entire sport of baseball. There was huge anticipation and speculation about where Bryce would end up.

Ultimately, he signed a staggering 13-year, $330 million contract with the Philadelphia Phillies, one of the largest contracts in the history of professional sports. The decision wasn't just about the money for Bryce. He wanted a long-term contract with a team where he could build a legacy. He wanted a city where he could raise his family. And he found that in Philadelphia.

In Philadelphia, Bryce has continued to impress. His powerful swing, lightning-fast speed, and exceptional fielding abilities keep fans on the edge of their seats. But perhaps what sets Bryce apart the most is his unwavering passion for the game. He plays hard every single game, and you can see the sheer joy he experiences when he's on the field.

Off the field, Bryce has also made an impact. He is often involved in charity work and is a strong advocate for children's health and education. He understands that with his fame and success comes the responsibility to give back and make a difference in the community.

Bryce Harper's journey to the Major Leagues is a story of determination, hard work, and a deep love for baseball. He's a reminder to all young players that no matter how much talent you have, you always have to keep working and striving to get better.

As we close this chapter on Bryce Harper, it's exciting to think about what's to come. After all, he's still in the prime of his career. There will be more home runs, more spectacular plays, and more memorable moments. But whatever happens, one thing is certain - Bryce Harper will always give his all to the game he loves.

And for all the young readers out there, dreaming of stepping onto the diamond and making their own mark on the sport, Bryce's story is a powerful reminder that with passion, hard work, and a love for the game, anything is possible.

Just remember - like Bryce, you're not just playing a game. You're following a dream. And that makes every swing, every catch, every run worth it. After all, as Bryce Harper would tell you, this is more than just a game. This is baseball.

# Chapter Fifteen:
# Gehrig and Ruth: The
# Unbreakable Bond

Our story begins in the roaring 20s, an era known for its jazz music, flapper dresses, and a national fascination with baseball. This was a time when the sport was becoming more than just a game; it was becoming a significant part of American culture. Two figures, in particular, stood out during this time - Babe Ruth and Lou Gehrig. They played for the New York Yankees, and their friendship, rivalry, and mutual respect created an unbreakable bond that would forever change the sport.

George Herman Ruth Jr., known to the world as Babe Ruth or "The Bambino," was already a legend in the baseball world. He began his career as a pitcher for the Boston Red Sox but later became famous as an outfielder for the Yankees. Ruth's larger-than-life personality, charismatic charm, and exceptional talent made him a beloved figure. He was known for his record-breaking home runs and was the star player the Yankees needed to attract larger crowds to their new stadium, which would later be known as "The House That Ruth Built."

Lou Gehrig, on the other hand, was a quieter and more reserved figure. Born in New York to German immigrant parents, Gehrig was a diligent, hardworking man both on and off the field. He had played football and studied engineering at Columbia University before joining the Yankees. He soon became known as the "Iron Horse" for his strength and durability. Gehrig played in a record-setting 2,130 consecutive games, a record that stood for 56 years.

The pair first played together in 1923, when Gehrig joined the Yankees. From the beginning, it was clear that these two men, despite their different personalities, shared a deep respect for each other and the game. They both had an undeniable passion for baseball and an impressive ability to hit home runs. This dynamic duo soon dominated the sport, thrilling fans with their extraordinary performances.

Ruth, with his exuberant personality, was the perfect foil to Gehrig's quiet, steady demeanor. They often batted back-to-back in the Yankees' lineup, a strategy that proved incredibly successful. The duo led the team to multiple World Series titles, becoming the heart and soul of the Yankees.

However, the friendship between Ruth and Gehrig wasn't always smooth sailing. There were rumors of a feud between them, sparked by a misunderstanding at a birthday party for Gehrig's mother. Despite this, their bond remained strong. Their respect for each other as players never wavered, and they managed to mend their relationship before Gehrig's untimely retirement due to a disease that now bears his name.

The decade of the 1920s was an absolute marvel in the world of baseball, primarily because of Ruth and Gehrig. The Yankees, under their influence, were virtually unstoppable, and the pair was known as the heart of the "Murderers' Row," a nickname for the formidable Yankee batting lineup of the time. Ruth and Gehrig didn't just make a great team; they shaped an era of baseball history.

Ruth, with his prodigious power, was the symbol of the live-ball era. He wasn't just a home run hitter; he was the home run hitter. His swing was a blend of power and grace, a spectacle that left fans in awe and adversaries in despair. He amassed record-breaking stats, but it was his love for the game and the fans that made him an enduring icon. Always quick with a joke and a smile, Ruth was a charmer both on and off the field.

Gehrig, in comparison, was Ruth's polar opposite in terms of personality. He wasn't the kind of player who sought the limelight. Instead, Gehrig was the embodiment of consistency, a player who showed up day after day, performing his role to the best of his ability. He was a steady force in the Yankees' lineup, providing balance to Ruth's flamboyance. Gehrig's record for consecutive games played, a testament to his resilience and determination, is still considered one of the most remarkable achievements in sports history.

The relationship between Ruth and Gehrig wasn't just one of mutual respect; it was also one of competition. Both men continually pushed each other to achieve more, to reach new heights in their careers. Ruth's power-hitting prowess motivated Gehrig, who in turn inspired Ruth with his unwavering consistency. Their rivalry, however, never spilled into animosity. They were competitive, yes, but they also understood that they were part of something bigger, something special.

Ruth was the first to exit the stage. He retired in 1935, leaving behind a legacy that few could hope to match. His departure marked the end of an era, but also the beginning of a new one. Gehrig was now the leader of the Yankees, the one carrying the torch. He continued to perform exceptionally, maintaining the team's high standards even in Ruth's absence.

However, tragedy struck in the form of a disease that was as relentless as Gehrig himself. He was diagnosed with amyotrophic lateral sclerosis (ALS), now commonly known as Lou Gehrig's disease. This debilitating condition would eventually force Gehrig to retire, but not before one of the most poignant moments in sports history.

In the summer of 1939, Gehrig was visibly weakening. His performance was suffering, and what was even more troubling, so was his health. It became clear that something was seriously wrong, and after a series of medical examinations, Gehrig was diagnosed with ALS. The news shook the world of baseball. It seemed unthinkable that a player as strong and enduring as Gehrig could be struck down in such a way.

Despite the heartbreaking diagnosis, Gehrig chose to face his condition with the same resilience and determination that had defined his baseball career. On July 4, 1939, Lou Gehrig Appreciation Day was held at Yankee Stadium. The stands were packed with fans and fellow players, all there to honor the man who had given so much to the sport.

Gehrig, standing on the field he had played on for so many years, delivered what is now known as his "Luckiest Man" speech. His words were filled with gratitude and humility, and they echoed around the stadium, reaching the hearts of everyone present. It was a moment of incredible strength and poise, a testament to Gehrig's character.

"I consider myself the luckiest man on the face of the earth," Gehrig said, standing amidst a sea of applauding fans. These words have since become synonymous with courage in the face of adversity. Gehrig, even in his toughest moment, chose to see the positive, to appreciate the journey he had been on.

Babe Ruth, upon hearing of Gehrig's condition, was deeply affected. Despite their differences, they shared a bond that went beyond their time together on the field. Ruth was present at Gehrig's farewell speech, standing beside his former teammate in a show of solidarity and friendship. Their shared history, the battles they had fought together, had forged an unbreakable bond between them.

The enduring image of Ruth and Gehrig, arms wrapped around each other on that fateful day, has since become a symbol of their remarkable relationship. It was a poignant moment, a goodbye not just from Gehrig, but from an era of baseball that Ruth and Gehrig had so distinctly shaped.

Gehrig passed away two years later, but his legacy, like Ruth's, lived on. The two of them, Ruth with his larger-than-life personality and Gehrig with his humble determination, had changed baseball forever. They were different in so many ways, but together, they formed one of the greatest duos the sport has ever seen. Their stories are reminders of the power of perseverance, the importance of friendship, and the love of the game that united them in their remarkable journeys.

So, as we close this chapter, we do so with a nod to these two legends, to their incredible bond, and to the timeless tales of courage and camaraderie that they left behind. The story of Babe Ruth and Lou Gehrig serves as a reminder to us all: regardless of our differences, it's the shared love for what we do that truly creates an unbreakable bond. And that is indeed a lesson worth taking away from the glorious history of baseball.

# Chapter Sixteen:
# The Kid: Ken Griffey Jr.'s
# Amazing Career

L ong before he was known as "The Kid," Ken Griffey Jr. was just a boy with a dream. A dream that was fostered in the energetic and bustling world of Major League Baseball. Born on November 21, 1969, in Donora, Pennsylvania, a town that also produced the great Stan Musial, Griffey was destined for the diamond. His father, Ken Griffey Sr., was a professional baseball player, and young Griffey Jr. spent his formative years in major league clubhouses, watching, learning, and falling in love with the game.

His childhood was a unique blend of the ordinary and extraordinary. Like many kids, he played youth baseball, developing his skills and fostering a deep love for the game. But unlike most, his father was a key player for the Cincinnati Reds, a member of the famed Big Red Machine. This gave young Griffey a firsthand look at the world of professional baseball, an experience that undoubtedly influenced and shaped him.

Griffey was a natural, and he quickly distinguished himself on the field. At Moeller High School in Cincinnati, he became a two-time national high school player of the year. He was the number one overall pick by the Seattle Mariners in the 1987 amateur draft, a selection that would change the fate of the franchise and set Griffey on a path towards greatness.

The Kid made his major league debut in 1989, at the tender age of 19. He singled in his first at-bat, a clear sign of the greatness that was to come. In his rookie year, Griffey showcased his incredible talent, hitting 16 home runs and driving in 61 runs. He quickly became a fan favorite, with his infectious grin, backwards cap, and astonishing athletic abilities.

Throughout his tenure with the Mariners, Junior showcased his wide-ranging abilities, becoming one of the most comprehensive players in the league. From his Gold Glove-worthy catches to his mighty swings that sent baseballs soaring out of the park, Griffey Jr. was a highlight reel unto himself.

However, his exceptional talent on the field wasn't the only thing that set Griffey Jr. apart. His signature backwards cap became a symbol of his playful nature and unique style. More than that, it was a nod to his father. Ken Griffey Sr. would wear his cap backward during batting practice, and Junior adopted the habit in his youth, carrying it with him throughout his professional career.

In 2000, Griffey Jr. made the decision to move closer to home, joining the Cincinnati Reds, the same team where his father had achieved significant success. It was an emotional move, filled with the promise of playing in front of his hometown crowd and creating new, unforgettable moments on the field.

In Cincinnati, Griffey Jr. continued to amaze, even though injuries began to slow him down. Still, he kept striving, kept playing, and never lost his love for the game. His tenacity was a testament to his character and demonstrated the same level of grit and determination that had seen him through his early years.

Despite the injuries, Griffey Jr. reached a significant milestone during his time with the Reds, hitting his 500th and 600th career home runs. These achievements only added to his legacy as one of the greatest to ever play the game.

Towards the end of his career, Griffey Jr. returned to Seattle, reuniting with the team and fans where he'd first become a superstar. He retired in 2010, leaving behind a legacy of excellence, integrity, and a love for the game that remained unwavering throughout his 22-season career.

His career was filled with jaw-dropping moments and achievements. He hit 630 home runs, was a 13-time All-Star, a 10-time Gold Glove winner, and the 1997 American League MVP. His smooth, seemingly effortless swing became the stuff of legend, as did his fearless and acrobatic catches in center field.

But perhaps one of the most remarkable aspects of Griffey's career was his relationship with his father. In 1990, Ken Griffey Sr., who was still an active player, signed with the Mariners, making them one of the few father-son duos to play on the same team. On September 14 of that year, they hit back-to-back home runs, an unprecedented event in Major League history. It was a testament to their close bond, the influence of Sr. on Jr., and the unique trajectory of Griffey's life and career.

Despite his impressive accomplishments, Griffey's career was not without challenges. Injuries took a toll on his performance and his playing time, but through it all, Griffey demonstrated a resilience and love for the game that endeared him to fans even more.

His infectious smile, backwards cap, and dazzling athleticism on the field earned him the affectionate moniker "The Kid." But more than that, his determination, resilience, and pure love for the game resonated with fans of all ages. Griffey played baseball with a joy and exuberance that harked back to childhood games of catch and neighborhood pick-up games. He reminded fans why they fell in love with baseball in the first place.

When Griffey was inducted into the Baseball Hall of Fame in 2016, he did so with a record-setting 99.32% of the vote, a fitting testament to his incredible impact on the sport. His speech, much like his career, was filled with genuine emotion and a deep appreciation for the game of baseball.

The story of Ken Griffey Jr. is one of talent, tenacity, and overcoming adversity. Like many athletes, his career was not devoid of struggles. Injuries hampered him repeatedly, most notably during his stint with the Cincinnati Reds. It was during these times that his determination was truly tested, as he fought back from each setback with a tenacity that was every bit as remarkable as his athletic talent.

Griffey's enduring legacy goes beyond his batting average, home runs, or Golden Glove awards. It lies in his character, both on and off the field. He was known for his grace, sportsmanship, and humility. He honored the game by playing it with joy and respect, never forgetting the boyhood dream that he was living out.

As a testament to his character, Griffey never got entangled in the steroid scandals that plagued Major League Baseball during his era. When asked about it, he simply said, "I want to be able to say that I did it the right way. I want to be able to look my kids in the eye and say, 'Dad did it the right way'." His words echoed the integrity that underscored his career.

Ken Griffey Jr.'s story can't be separated from his relationship with his father. Ken Griffey Sr. was not just a father, but a mentor, role model, and teammate. Their bond was showcased in the unique experience of playing together in the Major Leagues, a moment that highlighted their deep connection. The senior Griffey, a three-time All-Star in his own right, imparted his wisdom, work ethic, and love for the game to his son.

One of the most memorable moments in their shared baseball history came on September 14, 1990. In a game against the California Angels, father and son hit back-to-back home runs, an achievement that remains unmatched in baseball history. It was a moment that encapsulated their connection, their talent, and their mutual love for the game.

Ken Griffey Jr.'s story serves as an inspiration to young and old alike. His story is a testament to the power of dreams, the importance of perseverance, and the enduring value of integrity. As a player, he brought a youthful exuberance to the game, reminding everyone watching that at its heart, baseball is a game, meant to be enjoyed. He played with passion, respect, and an unmistakable joy, attributes that he continues to carry into his life post-retirement.

As we delve into the extraordinary life and career of 'The Kid', let's remember his contributions to baseball. From his unrivaled talent to his unblemished integrity, and his unbreakable bond with his father, Ken Griffey Jr.'s story is truly one for the ages. It's a story of baseball, family, and the love of the game that continues to inspire future generations. So here's to 'The Kid', who reminded us all to love the game, play with joy, and reach for the stars. His legacy is one that will be admired and remembered for generations to come in the world of baseball and beyond.

# Chapter Seventeen:
# From Mound to Desk: The
# Inspiring Transition of Jim Abbott

The story of Jim Abbott is a testament to resilience, determination, and unyielding ambition. It's a story that starts in Flint, Michigan, moves to the pitching mound of Yankee Stadium, and ends up in an inspiring post-baseball career that continues to motivate and inspire.

Born on September 19, 1967, Jim Abbott was different from other kids in one very noticeable way: he was born without a right hand. But what could have been seen as a setback was only a stepping stone for Jim. His parents encouraged him to live life like any other child and, with their support, Jim started to play sports. He played not just baseball, but also basketball and quarterbacked his high school football team. But it was baseball where he truly shone.

On the baseball field, Abbott defied all odds. He learned to expertly switch his glove between his left and residual right arm while on the mound. He would balance the glove on the end of his right arm, throw a pitch with his left, and then quickly switch the glove onto his left hand in case the ball was hit his way. It was a unique sight and his skill was an inspiration to many.

In high school, Abbott was an excellent student and an exceptional pitcher. After a successful career at Flint Central High School, he had the opportunity to take his talents to the next level. He was drafted by the Toronto Blue Jays right out of high school, but instead, he decided to accept a scholarship to the University of Michigan, where he would have the opportunity to both play baseball and continue his education.

At Michigan, Abbott was a force to be reckoned with on the baseball field. He led the Wolverines to two Big Ten Championships and in 1987, he even won the prestigious Golden Spikes Award, given annually to the best amateur baseball player in the country.

During his time in college, Abbott also had the honor of representing his country. He was the starting pitcher for Team USA at the 1988 Summer Olympics in Seoul, South Korea. Jim was instrumental in securing a gold medal for the United States, becoming a national hero in the process.

After his collegiate career, Jim was the 8th overall pick by the California Angels in the 1988 Major League Baseball draft. He bypassed the minor leagues, making his professional debut in the majors, a rare feat. As a rookie, Abbott posted a respectable record and was even named to the All-Rookie Team.

Despite his initial success, Abbott's journey in the Major Leagues was far from smooth. He faced slumps, and even periods of self-doubt, but his unwavering resilience would always see him through.

In 1991, his third year in the Major Leagues, Abbott posted an impressive 18 wins against 11 losses, with an equally impressive 2.89 Earned Run Average. This was his best season yet and earned him a third-place finish in the Cy Young Award voting, the award given annually to the best pitcher in each league.

After four years with the Angels, Abbott was traded to the New York Yankees before the start of the 1993 season. It was here that he would achieve one of his career highlights. On September 4, 1993, in a game against the Cleveland Indians, Jim Abbott, the pitcher born without a right hand, threw a no-hitter, one of the most outstanding achievements in baseball.

The no-hitter was a career-defining moment. Abbott was on top of the world. But as is often the case in sports, highs are often followed by lows. The following seasons were some of the toughest in his career. His performance declined, he was traded multiple times, and he even spent some time in the minor leagues.

Abbott officially retired from professional baseball in 1999. Despite the ups and downs, his career was nothing short of inspiring. In total, he spent ten seasons in the Major Leagues, played for four different teams, and left an indelible mark on the sport.

But for Abbott, life did not stop after baseball. He transitioned to a successful career as a motivational speaker, using his unique story to inspire others to overcome their own obstacles. His message was always one of positivity and determination: "It's not the disability that defines you," he would often say, "it's how you deal with the challenges the disability presents you with."

In his speeches, he talked about his life, his struggles, and his triumphs. He talked about how he never saw himself as having a disability, but rather, just a unique challenge to overcome. He stressed the importance of a positive mindset, determination, and the ability to adapt, all lessons he learned from his own life.

Despite his newfound career, Abbott's love for baseball never waned. He stayed connected with the sport, frequently attending games and participating in charity events. He even took up coaching at a youth level, sharing his wisdom with budding young players who admired his grit and passion.

On the speaking circuit, Abbott wasn't just sharing his life story; he was transforming lives. From young athletes to corporate executives, his audience was captivated by his unyielding spirit. His speeches weren't merely about baseball; they were about life, about facing challenges head-on, about not letting limitations define you, and about realizing your potential.

Even outside the realm of sports, his story resonated with many. He often shared a mantra he'd learned from his parents:

"It's not what happens to you; it's what you do about it." This message echoed with everyone who'd faced hardship or adversity.

In 2007, Abbott was awarded the Tony Conigliaro Award, an annual recognition by the Major League Baseball for the player who best overcomes an obstacle and adversity through the attributes of spirit, determination, and courage. This was a testament not only to his baseball career but also his life journey.

Abbott also wrote a memoir titled "Imperfect: An Improbable Life," where he shares his remarkable journey from a child who loved sports but had to adapt to his circumstances, to a Major League Baseball player and Olympic gold medalist. The book, like his speeches, is filled with inspiring messages about overcoming obstacles, and the belief that you can achieve anything if you set your mind to it.

The year 2014 marked another significant milestone in Abbott's journey. His number 31 was retired by the University of Michigan, where his journey to stardom began. This was an honor that touched Abbott deeply as it brought his incredible journey full circle. "Michigan was a dream come true for me," he said during the ceremony, showing just how much the university and his time there meant to him.

His story is now used by many as a source of motivation and strength. Parents share it with their children, coaches with their athletes, teachers with their students. In classrooms, his autobiography is used to teach children about resilience, perseverance, and the belief in oneself.

Jim Abbott might have hung up his baseball cleats, but his impact on the world has been far from retiring. From a small boy in Flint, Michigan, dreaming of playing in the Major Leagues, to a renowned motivational speaker, his journey has been nothing short of awe-inspiring. He continues to inspire, motivate, and change lives with his story.

Indeed, Jim Abbott is not only a baseball icon but also a symbol of resilience and determination, a testament to the human spirit's ability to overcome obstacles. His story serves as a powerful reminder that no matter what challenges we face, we all have the power within us to rise above them and achieve greatness.

And so, his legacy continues, not just on the baseball diamond, but in countless hearts and minds worldwide. From mound to desk, from baseball to motivational speaking, the inspiring transition of Jim Abbott remains a shining beacon of courage, perseverance, and the indomitable human spirit. His story continues to inspire, reminding us all of the incredible power of never giving up.

# Chapter Eighteen:

# The Queen of the Diamond: Mo'ne Davis Takes the World by Storm

L et me take you back in time, to the vibrant city of Philadelphia in the year 2001, where our story begins. Amidst the city's towering skyscrapers and historic landmarks, a star was born. A star whose radiant light would, in time, illuminate the world of baseball, a sport long ruled by men. Her name was Mo'ne Davis.

Even as a young child, Mo'ne had a fiery spirit and an unyielding determination that set her apart from the rest. There was a certain charm about her, a sparkle in her eyes that spoke of unexplored potential and untamed dreams. Sports, from basketball to soccer, were her passion, but it was baseball that truly ignited her soul.

In her small hands, a baseball seemed to come alive. Her throws were precise and swift, her catches deft and graceful, and her batting strong and accurate. She was like a whirlwind on the diamond, fierce, unpredictable, and immensely talented.

When she was still quite young, her extraordinary talent caught the eye of Steve Bandura, a local Little League coach. Watching her effortlessly navigate the field, he knew he had discovered a raw gem. Mo'ne, with her fiery determination and intuitive understanding of the game, was an asset he could not ignore. He took her under his wing, nurturing her talent and shaping her into an extraordinary player.

Life, however, had its fair share of obstacles waiting for Mo'ne. Skeptics doubted her abilities, critics raised their eyebrows, and some even dismissed her dream simply because she was a girl playing a 'boys' sport. But Mo'ne was not one to be deterred. With every discouraging word, her resolve only grew stronger. She pushed harder, trained longer, and played with an unyielding spirit that would eventually silence her detractors.

When Mo'ne was just thirteen years old, she did something truly spectacular. Her team, the Taney Dragons, made it to the Little League World Series in 2014, largely thanks to Mo'ne's incredible pitching. With her 70-mile-per-hour fastball, a pitch most boys her age could only dream of mastering, Mo'ne led her team to victory. In doing so, she became the first girl to earn a win and pitch a shutout in Little League World Series history.

Mo'ne was no longer just a player; she was a symbol of resilience, a beacon of hope for every girl who was ever told that they couldn't or shouldn't play baseball. Her talent was undeniable, her influence far-reaching, and her story truly inspirational. Every time she stepped onto the diamond, she was challenging norms, breaking barriers, and rewriting the rules of the game. Mo'ne was proving to the world that baseball was a sport for everyone, regardless of gender.

Her historical achievement at the Little League World Series did not go unnoticed. The world watched in awe as this young girl made waves in a sport that had long been a boys' club. She captured hearts, inspired millions, and most importantly, she shattered stereotypes. In recognition of her remarkable accomplishments, she graced the cover of Sports Illustrated, a prestigious honor never before bestowed upon a Little Leaguer.

As we dive deeper into Mo'ne's story, let us remember the impact she had, not just on the game, but on the world. She reminded us that with courage and persistence, we can overcome any obstacle, defy any stereotype, and rewrite the narrative, no matter what it may be. Mo'ne Davis was, and always will be, the Queen of the Diamond.

On August 15, 2014, when the Little League World Series began, the world saw firsthand the impressive power Mo'ne Davis wielded. She was a dominant force on the field, a dynamo that seized the attention of spectators and players alike. Every time she took the mound, the world held its collective breath, anticipating her next feat.

Her first game was against the team from Nashville. With a combination of fastballs and sliders, Mo'ne struck out eight batters and gave up only two hits, achieving a complete-game shutout. The magnitude of her accomplishment began to echo across the globe - a girl had claimed victory in the Little League World Series. Not only had she played, she had dominated. Mo'ne had etched her name in the annals of baseball history, and she was just getting started.

In her second game, the Dragons faced the potent team from Las Vegas, and though they didn't win, Mo'ne's performance was still commendable. In fact, her brilliance shone even brighter against the odds. Despite the setback, Mo'ne and her team rallied, refusing to let one loss define their journey. They continued to push through, to fight, to dream.

Mo'ne's display of prowess in the World Series caught the eye of baseball enthusiasts, sports pundits, and media outlets worldwide. She was celebrated as a testament to the potential of female athletes in traditionally male sports. She was invited on talk shows, profiled by news outlets, and even received commendations from well-known athletes, celebrities, and politicians. From Kevin Durant to Ellen DeGeneres and former President Barack Obama, the praise for Mo'ne Davis was universal.

Even with all the attention, Mo'ne never let the fame cloud her humble nature. She was still the determined young girl from Philadelphia who loved baseball. In interviews, she would often speak about her love for the sport, her teammates, and her ambitions for the future. She was a shining example of modesty and grace under the global spotlight, an inspiration for many young athletes.

Her story was more than just baseball; it was about breaking barriers, proving critics wrong, and inspiring girls worldwide. Mo'ne Davis made it known that baseball wasn't just a sport for boys. Girls could play, dominate, and make history too. She showed the world that given the opportunity, girls could shine just as brightly as boys, if not brighter.

But Mo'ne's journey didn't end with the Little League World Series. She continued to inspire, to break boundaries, and to challenge the norms, both on and off the field. Even after the end of the series, Mo'ne's passion for sports remained a defining part of her life. Her sporting journey continued, her influence only grew, and her story only became more remarkable.

Off the field, Mo'ne carried herself with a maturity and grace that belied her age. Even as her fame grew, she always made it clear that her accomplishments were due to hard work and a supportive team. She credited her coaches for teaching her everything she knew and thanked her parents and older brothers for encouraging her love for sports.

Despite the fame and attention, Mo'ne remained focused on her academics. She understood the importance of education and balanced her schoolwork and training expertly. She was as much a star in the classroom as she was on the baseball diamond.

After her monumental stint in the Little League World Series, Mo'ne continued to play baseball, though she also began to branch out into other sports. She joined her school's soccer and basketball teams, proving herself to be a gifted all-around athlete. She once admitted that basketball was her first love and she aspired to play for the University of Connecticut, one of the best women's basketball programs in the country.

Throughout her journey, Mo'ne inspired countless girls and boys worldwide. She showed everyone that they could defy stereotypes and that they should chase their dreams, no matter how impossible they seemed. Mo'ne's path was not easy, and she had to overcome several obstacles, including prejudice, doubt, and intense pressure. But she weathered the storm with resilience and an unshakeable belief in herself.

Mo'ne's legacy extends far beyond the diamond. She used her platform to raise awareness about the importance of equality in sports. She believed that every girl should have the chance to play, regardless of the sport. Her success highlighted the need for more support and representation for female athletes in all sports, not just baseball.

By the time she was 15, Mo'ne had already begun writing the next chapter of her life. She released a memoir titled "Mo'ne Davis: Remember My Name", in which she shared her journey in her own words. It became a New York Times Bestseller, further cementing her legacy.

The story of Mo'ne Davis is a tale of determination, skill, and grace. She's not only a trailblazer in the world of sports but also an inspiration for countless young girls who dream of making it big in the world of athletics. Mo'ne showed us that you could overcome any obstacle with hard work, perseverance, and a little bit of self-belief.

# Chapter Nineteen:
# The Two-Way Sensation: Shohei Ohtani's Journey from Japan to the Big Leagues

In a small city in Northern Japan, there was a boy who loved baseball. His name was Shohei Ohtani, and he dreamed of becoming a Major League Baseball player one day. Shohei was no ordinary baseball fan. He was not just a batter or a pitcher; he wanted to be both. He wanted to be a two-way player, an anomaly in the modern world of baseball.

Shohei was born in the town of Oshu, Japan, in 1994. He was the eldest of three children, and his parents were factory workers who loved sports. From a young age, his father nurtured his baseball skills, and his mother, a former badminton player, encouraged his love for sports. By the time he was in high school, Shohei had grown to be a tall and powerful athlete. His speed, power, and ability to throw lightning-fast pitches made him a sensation in Japanese high school baseball.

Shohei's talent did not go unnoticed. In fact, the Hokkaido Nippon-Ham Fighters, a team in Nippon Professional Baseball (NPB), Japan's major league, drafted him right out of high school. They promised to allow him to be a two-way player, a rarity in professional baseball, and it was an opportunity he couldn't pass up. The Fighters recognized his rare talent and the raw power that lay within him.

In his first season with the Fighters, Ohtani showed signs of his extraordinary talent. He could hit, run, and throw at an exceptional level. In 2016, he had a breakout year. Not only did he hit .322 with 22 home runs and 67 RBIs in just 104 games, but he also posted a 1.86 ERA with 174 strikeouts in 140 innings on the mound. He was named both the league's best pitcher and its best designated hitter, and he led the Fighters to a championship victory. His performance was historic, and it attracted the attention of Major League Baseball scouts. He was living his dream, but his aspirations were higher. He wanted to play in the MLB.

Meanwhile, across the Pacific, Major League Baseball teams were taking notice of the young Japanese phenom. His ability to throw a baseball at over 100 miles per hour and hit it over 500 feet was astounding. They saw a talent that was rare, a talent that could potentially change the way baseball was played. The bidding war to bring Shohei Ohtani to America was fierce, but in the end, it was the Los Angeles Angels who won the race.

Moving to America was a big leap for Shohei. He had to overcome language barriers, cultural differences, and the physical toll of playing at the highest level of the sport. He had to adjust his game to face some of the best baseball players in the world. But he was determined to make it work. He had a dream to fulfill, after all.

In his debut season with the Angels in 2018, he lived up to the hype, and then some. Despite an injury that limited his pitching, he had a fantastic season at the plate, hitting .285 with 22 home runs and 61 RBIs in just 104 games, earning him the American League Rookie of the Year award. His performances as both a pitcher and a hitter thrilled fans and reminded many of Babe Ruth, the last player to excel in both roles.

It wasn't all smooth sailing, though. He faced significant challenges along the way. A major injury required him to have Tommy John surgery, sidelining his pitching for a while. He had to adapt to new pitching styles and techniques that American baseball presented. But through it all, Shohei stayed committed to his goal.

Once he was able to return to the mound in 2020, he worked hard to find the same kind of success he'd experienced at the plate. It took a lot of time, a lot of training, and a lot of patience, but Shohei never gave up. He honed his control, improved his mechanics, and got better with each game he played.

The 2021 season was a remarkable one for Shohei. He showcased his exceptional abilities as both a pitcher and a hitter, reminding everyone why he was called a two-way sensation. Shohei became the first player to be selected to the All-Star game as both a pitcher and a hitter. His feats were unprecedented, drawing comparisons to the legendary Babe Ruth once again. He was not just living up to his promise; he was exceeding expectations.

Off the field, Shohei was making strides as well. He was learning English, adapting to American culture, and becoming a beloved figure in his new home. He charmed fans with his humility, work ethic, and love for the game. He signed autographs, took pictures, and always made time for his fans. The people loved him, and he loved them right back.

There's a particular instance that stands out about Shohei's connection with his fans. It was during a home game, and Shohei was signing autographs for a group of young fans. A boy, no older than eight, managed to catch Shohei's attention. He was carrying a picture of Shohei that he had drawn himself. It showed Shohei as a superhero, complete with a cape and a baseball bat in hand. The boy handed the picture to Shohei, his eyes wide with excitement. Shohei looked at the picture, then at the boy, and then signed the picture with a smile. He ruffled the boy's hair and thanked him. That moment, that connection, was what baseball was all about.

Shohei Ohtani's journey from Japan to the Big Leagues is one of perseverance, dedication, and a love for the game. It's a story of a boy who dared to dream big and had the courage to chase those dreams. Shohei's tale is a testament to the fact that with hard work, determination, and a little bit of talent, anything is possible.

The next chapters of Shohei's career are still being written. He has many more seasons ahead of him, many more games to play, and many more records to break. But no matter what happens in the future, Shohei Ohtani has already made his mark on baseball. He's shown the world that a player can be a top-tier pitcher and a powerful hitter at the same time. He's shown us that you can be whatever you want to be if you're willing to put in the work.

So, the next time you watch Shohei Ohtani pitch a shutout or hit a home run, remember the journey he took to get there. Remember the boy from Oshu who dared to dream. Remember his love for the game, his dedication, and his never-give-up attitude. Because Shohei Ohtani is not just a baseball player; he's a testament to the power of dreams and the beauty of baseball.

# Chapter Twenty:
# The Great One: The Story of
# Roberto Clemente

Roberto Clemente, the first Latin American player to be inducted into the Baseball Hall of Fame, was known for his exceptional baseball skills, his humanitarian efforts, and his dignified character. His story is one of overcoming racial prejudice, setting new standards in the sport, and leaving a lasting legacy that transcends the baseball diamond.

Born on August 18, 1934, in Carolina, Puerto Rico, Clemente was the youngest of seven children. From a young age, Clemente showed a deep interest in baseball. Despite his family's limited resources, he often improvised with homemade equipment to feed his passion for the sport. His mother once said that Clemente could hit a kernel of corn with a stick.

Growing up in Puerto Rico, Clemente faced many economic challenges. His family's poor circumstances forced him to work alongside his father in the sugarcane fields to help supplement the family's income. But the harsh circumstances of his upbringing only fueled his determination to succeed.

His talent on the field caught the attention of scouts from major league baseball. In 1952, at the age of 18, Clemente was playing in the Puerto Rican Professional Baseball League when he was noticed by the Brooklyn Dodgers. The Dodgers signed him to a minor league contract and he played for their Triple-A team, the Montreal Royals, before being selected by the Pittsburgh Pirates in the rookie draft in 1954.

The early years of his career were challenging. He faced racism and language barriers in the United States, something he had not encountered in Puerto Rico. Despite these hurdles, Clemente's dedication to the sport remained unwavering. He quickly became a standout player for the Pirates, playing right field and gaining a reputation for his strong and accurate throwing arm.

Over the next 18 seasons, Clemente would transform the Pirates into a championship team. He led the Pirates to victory in the 1960 and 1971 World Series, was named the National League's Most Valuable Player in 1966, and became a twelve-time Gold Glove Award winner. His .317 lifetime batting average and his 3,000 career hits put him among the elite in baseball history.

However, his accomplishments on the field were only one aspect of Clemente's legacy. Off the field, he was known for his charity work and commitment to social justice. He strongly believed in giving back to the community and frequently participated in charitable events in both Puerto Rico and the United States.

One of Clemente's most important contributions was his advocacy for greater recognition and respect for Latin American players in major league baseball. He often spoke out against the prejudice they faced and worked tirelessly to promote understanding and acceptance among his fellow players and the fans.

Clemente's life was tragically cut short on December 31, 1972, when a plane he had chartered to deliver aid to earthquake victims in Nicaragua crashed shortly after takeoff. His sudden death shocked the world and left a profound impact on the sport of baseball.

As Roberto Clemente's playing days concluded with that tragic flight in 1972, his legacy was just beginning to shine brighter. His story remained, etched in the hearts of fans, fellow players, and generations of aspiring athletes. The Baseball Writers' Association of America, acknowledging his enormous contribution to the sport, waived their mandatory five-year waiting period, and Clemente was posthumously inducted into the Baseball Hall of Fame in 1973, becoming the first Latin American player to receive this honor.

But the Baseball Hall of Fame was not the only institution to honor Clemente. Major League Baseball also established the Roberto Clemente Award, given annually to the player who best exemplifies the sport through extraordinary character, community involvement, philanthropy, and positive contributions, both on and off the field. Each year, this award echoes Clemente's profound impact on baseball and society, recognizing the players who embody the same spirit of giving and perseverance that he did.

Roberto Clemente's legacy stretched beyond his incredible skill and stats; it was defined by the man he was — resolute, compassionate, and utterly devoted to serving his community. His journey from the sandy fields of Puerto Rico to the lush lawns of major league stadiums, and eventually to the hallowed halls of Cooperstown, is a testament to his indomitable spirit and unparalleled dedication.

In the world of baseball, there are many great players, many heroes, and many legends. But there are only a few who transcend the sport, who become symbols of courage, dignity, and humanity. Roberto Clemente was one such individual. Through his life, he demonstrated that one's true character is measured not by their athletic prowess but by their actions off the field, their ability to effect positive change, and their unwavering commitment to helping others.

Roberto Clemente's tale is far more than just a baseball story. It's a testament to the power of perseverance, the importance of integrity, and the enduring impact of using one's abilities to make a positive difference. His life and career serve as an enduring testament to what an individual can achieve when talent meets tenacity and when fame fuels a drive to give back.

From a young boy practicing with a makeshift glove in Puerto Rico to becoming an icon of the sport, Clemente's journey is a beacon of inspiration. It tells us that no matter where we come from or what challenges we face, with determination, grace, and a heart committed to helping others, we can make a difference.

And so, as the sun sets on the story of Roberto Clemente, his legacy continues to shine brightly, a guiding star in the vast expanse of baseball history. He remains "The Great One," not just in his time but for all time, inspiring generations past, present, and those yet to come. Through his life, Clemente illuminated a path showing us how sport can serve as a powerful platform for change and how a single individual can become an immortal symbol of resilience, kindness, and undying love for the game.